THE BIG BROTHER

A Story of Indian War

GEORGE CARY EGGLESTON

1st WORLD
LIBRARY
Literary Society

The Big Brother

George Cary Eggleston

© 1st World Library, 2007
PO Box 2211
Fairfield, IA 52556
www.1stworldlibrary.com
First Edition

LCCN: 2007930785

Softcover ISBN: 978-1-4218-4826-6
Hardcover ISBN: 978-1-4218-4729-0
eBook ISBN: 978-1-4218-4923-2

Purchase *"The Big Brother"*
as a traditional bound book at:
www.1stWorldLibrary.com/purchase.asp?ISBN=978-1-4218-4826-6

1st World Library is a literary, educational organization
dedicated to:

- Creating a free internet library of downloadable ebooks

- Hosting writing competitions and offering book publishing
scholarships.

Interested in more 1st World Library books? contact:
literacy@1stworldlibrary.com
Check us out at: www.1stworldlibrary.com

1ˢᵗ World Library Literary Society

Giving Back to the World

"If you want to work on the core problem, it's early school literacy."

- James Barksdale, former CEO of Netscape

"No skill is more crucial to the future of a child, or to a democratic and prosperous society, than literacy."

- Los Angeles Times

"Literacy... means far more than learning how to read and write... The aim is to transmit... knowledge and promote social participation."

- UNESCO

"Literacy is not a luxury, it is a right and a responsibility. If our world is to meet the challenges of the twenty-first century we must harness the energy and creativity of all our citizens."

- President Bill Clinton

"Parents should be encouraged to read to their children, and teachers should be equipped with all available techniques for teaching literacy, so the varying needs and capacities of individual kids can be taken into account."

- Hugh Mackay

CONTENTS

CHAPTER I

SINQUEFIELD

In the quiet days of peace and security in which we live it is difficult to imagine such a time of excitement as that at which our story opens, in the summer of 1813. From the beginning of that year, the Creek Indians in Alabama and Mississippi had shown a decided disposition to become hostile. In addition to the usual incentives to war which always exist where the white settlements border closely upon Indian territory, there were several special causes operating to bring about a struggle at that time. We were already at war with the British, and British agents were very active in stirring up trouble on our frontiers, knowing that nothing would so surely weaken the Americans as a general outbreak of Indian hostilities. Tecumseh, the great chief, had visited the Creeks, too, and had urged them to go on the war path, threatening them, in the event of their refusal, with the wrath of the Great Spirit. His appeals to their superstition were materially strengthened by the occurrence of an earthquake, which singularly enough, he had predicted, threatening that when he returned to his home he would stamp his foot and shake their houses down. Their own prophets, Francis and Singuista, had preached war, too, telling the Indians that their partial adoption of civilization, and their relations of friendship with the whites, were sorely displeasing to the Great Spirit, who would surely punish them if they did not immediately abandon the civilization and butcher the pale-faces. Francis predicted, also, that in the coming struggle no Indians would be killed, while the whites would be completely exterminated. All this was promised on condition that the Indians should become complete savages again, quitting all the habits of industry and thrift which they had been learning for some years past, and fighting mercilessly against all whites, sparing none.

All these things combined to bring on the war, and during the spring several raids were made by small bodies of the Indians, in which they were pretty severely punished by the whites. Finally a battle was fought at Burnt-corn, in July 1813, and this was the signal for the breaking out of the most terrible of all Indian wars,—the most terrible, because the savages engaged in it had learned from the whites how to fight, and because many of their chiefs were educated half-breeds, familiar with the country and with all the points of weakness on the part of the settlers. Stockade forts were built in various places, and in these the settlers took refuge, leaving their fields to grow as they might and their houses to be plundered and burned whenever the Indians should choose to visit them. The stockades were so built as to enclose several acres each, and strong block houses inside, furnished additional protection. Into these forts there came men, women, and children, from all parts of the country, each bringing as much food as possible, and each willing to lend a hand to the common defence and the common support.

On the 30th of August, the Indians attacked Fort Mims, one of the largest of the stockade stations, and after a desperate battle destroyed it, killing all but seventeen of the five hundred and fifty people who were living in it. The news of this terrible slaughter quickly spread over the country, and everybody knew now that a general war had begun, in which the Indians meant to destroy the whites utterly, not sparing even the youngest children.

Those who had remained on their farms now flocked in great numbers to the forts, and every effort was made to strengthen the defences at all points. The men, including all the boys who were large enough to point a gun and pull a trigger, were organized into companies and assigned to port-holes, in order that each might know where to go to do his part of the fighting whenever the Indians should come. Even those of the women who knew how to shoot, insisted upon being provided with guns and assigned to posts of duty. There was not only no use in flinching, but every one of them knew that whenever the fort should be attacked the only question to be decided was, "Shall we beat the savages off, or shall every man woman and child of us be butchered?" They could not run away, for there was nowhere to run, except into the hands of the merciless foe. The life of every one of them was involved in the defence of the forts, and each was, therefore, anxious to do all he could to make the defense a successful one. Their only hope was in desperate courage, and, being Americans, their courage was equal to the demand made upon it. It was not a civilized war, in which surrenders, and exchanges of prisoners, and treaties and flags of truce, or even neutrality offered any escape. It was a savage war, in which the Indians intended to kill all the whites, old and young, wherever they could find them. The people in the forts knew this, and they made their arrangements accordingly.

Now if the boys and girls who read this story will get their atlases and turn to the map of Alabama, they will find some points, the relative positions of which they must remember if they wish to understand fully the happenings with which we have to do. Just below the junction of the Alabama and Tombigbee rivers, on the east side of the stream, they will find the little town of Tensaw, and Fort Mims stood very near that place. The peninsula formed by the two rivers above their junction is now Clarke County, and almost exactly in its centre stands the village of Grove Hill. A mile or two to the north-east stood Fort Sinquefield. Fort White was several miles further west, and Fort Glass, afterwards called Fort Madison, stood fifteen miles south, at a point about three miles south of the present village of Suggsville. On the eastern side of the Alabama river is the town of Claiborne, and at a point about three miles below Claiborne the principal events of this story occurred. It will not hurt you, boys and girls, to learn a little accurate geography, by looking up these places before going on with the story, and if I were your schoolmaster, instead of your story teller, I should stop here to advise you always to look on the map for every town, river, lake, mountain or other geographical thing mentioned in any book or paper you read. I would advise you, too, if I were your schoolmaster, to add up all the figures given in books and newspapers, to see if the writers have made any mistakes; and it is a good plan too, to go at once to the dictionary when you meet a word you do not quite comprehend, or to the encyclopaedia or history, or whatever else is handy, whenever you read about anything and would like to know more about it. I say I should stop here to give you some such advice as this, if I were your schoolmaster. As I am not, however, I must go on with my story instead.

Within a mile or two of Fort Sinquefield lived a gentleman named Hardwicke. He was a widower with three children. Sam, the oldest of the three, was nearly seventeen; Tommy was eleven, and a little girl of seven years, named Judith, but called Judie, was the other. Mr. Hardwicke was a quiet, studious man, who had come to Alabama from Baltimore, not many years before, and since the death of his wife he had spent most of his time in his library, which was famous throughout the settlement on account of the wonderful number of books it contained. There were hardly any schools in Alabama in those days, and Mr. Hardwicke, being a man

George Cary Eggleston

of education and considerable wealth, gave up almost the whole of his time to his children, teaching them in doors and out, and directing them in their reading. It was understood that Sam would be sent north to attend College the next year, and meantime he had become a voracious reader. He read all sorts of books, and as he remembered and applied the things he learned from them, it was a common saying in the country round about, that "Sam Hardwicke knows pretty nearly everything." Of course that was not true, but he knew a good deal more than most of the men in the country, and better than all, he knew how very much there was for him yet to learn. A boy has learned the very best lesson of his life when he knows that he really does not know much; it is a lesson some people never learn at all. But books were not the only things Sam Hardwicke was familiar with. He could ride the worst horses in the country and shoot a rifle almost as well as Tandy Walker himself, and Tandy, as every reader of history knows, was the most famous rifleman, as well as the best guide and most daring scout in the whole south-west. Sam had hunted, too, over almost every inch of country within twenty miles around, trudging alone sometimes for a week or a fortnight before returning, and in this way he had learned to know the distances, the directions, and the nature of the country lying between different places,—a knowledge worth gaining by anybody, and especially valuable to a boy who lived in a frontier settlement. He was strong of limb and active as he was strong, and his "book knowledge," as the neighbors called it, served him many a good turn in the woods, when he was beset by difficulties.

Sam's father was one of the very last of the settlers to go into a fort. He remained at home as long as he could, and went to Fort Sinquefield at last, only when warned by an Indian who for some reason liked him, that he and his children's lives were in imminent danger. That was on the first of September, and when the Hardwicke family, black and white, were safely within the little fortress, there remained outside only two families, namely, those of Abner James and Ransom Kimball, who determined to remain one more night at Kimball's house, two miles from Sinquefield. That very night the Indians, under Francis the prophet, burned the house, killing twelve of the inmates. Five others escaped, and one of them, Isham Kimball, who was then a boy of sixteen, afterwards became Clerk of Clarke County, where he was still living in 1857.

CHAPTER II

THE STORMING OF SINQUEFIELD

When the news of the massacre at Kimball's reached Fort Glass, a detachment of ten men was sent out to recover the bodies, which they brought to Fort Sinquefield for burial. The graves were dug in a little valley three or four hundred yards from the fort, and all the people went out to attend the funeral. The services had just come to an end when the cry of "Indians! Indians!" was raised, and a body of warriors, under the prophet Francis, dashed down from behind a hill, upon the defenceless people, whose guns were inside the fort. The first impulse of every one was to catch up the little children and hasten inside the gates, but it was manifestly too late. The Indians were already nearer the fort than they, and were running with all their might, brandishing their knives and tomahawks, and yelling like demons.

There seemed no way of escape. Sam Hardwicke took little Judie up in his arms, and, quick as thought calculated the chances of reaching the fort. Clearly the only way in which he could possibly get there, was by leaving his little sister to her fate and running for his life. But Sam Hardwicke was not the sort of boy to do anything so cowardly as that. Abandoning the thought of getting to the fort, he called to Tom to follow him, and with Judie in his arms, he ran into a neighboring thicket, where the three, with Joe, a black boy of twelve or thirteen years who had followed them, concealed themselves in the bushes. Whether they had been seen by the Indians or not, they had no way of knowing, but their only hope of safety now lay in absolute stillness. They crouched down together and kept silence.

"What's we gwine to do here, I wonder," whispered the black boy. "Whar mus' we go, Mas Sam?"

Sam did not answer. He was too much absorbed in studying the situation to talk or even to listen. The Indians were coming down upon the white people from every side, and the only wonder was that Sam's little party had managed to find a gap in their line big enough to escape through.

"Be patient, Joe," said little Judie, in the calmest voice possible. "Brother Sam will take care of us. Give him time. He always does know what to do."

"Be still, Joe," said Sam. "If you talk that Indian'll see us," pointing to one not thirty steps distant, though Joe had not yet seen him.

A terrified "ugh!" was all the reply Joe could make.

Meantime the situation of the fort people was terrible. Cut off from the gates and unarmed, there seemed to be nothing for them to do except to meet death as bravely and calmly as they could. A young man named Isaac Harden happened to be near the gates, however, on horseback, and accompanied by a pack of about sixty hounds. And this young man, whose name has barely crept into a corner of history, was both a hero and a military genius, and he did right then and there, a deed as brilliant and as heroic as any other in history. Seeing the perilous position of the fort people, he raised himself in his stirrups and waving his hat, charged the savages *with his pack of dogs*, whooping and yelling after the manner of a

George Cary Eggleston

huntsman, and leading the fierce bloodhounds right into the ranks of the infuriated Indians. The dogs being trained to chase and seize any living thing upon which their master might set them, attacked the Indians furiously, Harden encouraging them and riding down group after group of the bewildered savages. Charging right and left with his dogs, he succeeded in putting the Indians for a time upon the defensive, thus giving the white people time to escape into the fort. When all were in except Sam's party and a Mrs. Phillips who was killed, Harden began looking about him for a chance to secure his own safety. His impetuosity had carried him clear through the Indian ranks, and the savages, having beaten the dogs off, turned their attention to the young cavalier who had balked them in the very moment of their victory. They were between him and the gates, hundreds against one. His dogs were killed or scattered, and he saw at a glance that there was little hope for him. The woods behind him were full of Indians, and so retreat was impossible. Turning his horse's head towards the gates, he plunged spurs into his side, and with a pistol in each hand, dashed through the savage ranks, firing as he went. Blowing a blast upon his horn to recall those of his dogs which were still alive, he escaped on foot into the fort, just in time to let the gate shut in the face of the foremost Indian. His horse, history tells us, was killed under him, and he had five bullet holes through his clothes, but his skin was unbroken.

Francis and his followers were balked but not beaten. Retiring for a few minutes behind the hill, they rallied and came again to the assault, more furiously than ever. Their savage instincts were thoroughly aroused by the unexpected defeat they had sustained in the very moment of their victory, and they were determined now to take the fort at any cost. Their plan of attack showed the skill of their leader, who was really a man of considerable ability in spite of his fanatical belief in his own prophetic gifts. He avoided both the errors usually committed by Indian leaders in storming fortified places. He refused, on the one hand, to let his men waste their powder and their time in desultory firing, and, on the other, he decided not to risk everything on the hazard of a single assault. His plan was to take the fort by storm, but the storming was to be done systematically. Dividing his force into two parts, he sent one to the attack, and held the other back in the hope that the first would gain a position so near the stockade as to make the assault of the second, led by himself, doubly sure of success. The plan was a good one, without doubt, and no man was better qualified than Francis to carry it out.

When the storming party came, the people in the fort were ready for it. Counting out the women and children, their numbers were not large, but they were a brave and determined set of men and boys, who knew very well in what kind of a struggle they were engaged. They reserved their fire until the Indians were within thirty yards of the fort, and then delivered it as rapidly as they could, taking care to waste none of it by random or careless shooting. The fort consisted, as all the border fortifications did, of a simple stockade, inside of which was a block-house for the protection of the women and children, and designed also as a sort of "last ditch," in which a desperate resistance could be made, even after the fort had been carried. The stockade was made of the trunks of pine-trees set on end in the ground, close together, but pierced at intervals with port-holes, through which the men of the garrison could fire. Such a stockade afforded an excellent protection against the bullets and the arrows of the Indians, and gave its defenders a great advantage over the assailing force, which must, of course, be exposed to a galling fire from the men behind the barriers. As the stockade was about fifteen feet high, climbing over it was almost wholly out of the question, and the only way to take the fort was to rush upon it with fence rails, stop up the port-holes immediately in front, and keep so close to the stockade as to escape the fire from points to the right and

George Cary Eggleston

left, while engaged in cutting down the timber barrier. If the Indians could do this, their superior numbers would enable them to rush in through the opening thus made, and then the block-house would be the only refuge left to the white people. The block-house was a building made of very large timbers, hewed square, laid close upon each other and notched to an exact fit at the ends. It had but one entrance, and that was near the top. This could be reached only by a ladder, and should the Indians gain access to the fort, the whites would retire, fighting, to this building, and when all were in, the ladder would be drawn in after them. From the port-holes of the block-house a fierce fire could be delivered, and as the square timbers were not easily set on fire, a body of Indians must be very determined indeed, if they succeeded in taking or destroying a block-house. At Fort Mims, however, they had done so, burning the house over the heads of the inmates.

The reader will understand, from this description of the fort, how possible it was for the people within it to withstand a very determined attack, and to inflict heavy loss upon the savages, without suffering much in their turn. Francis's men charged furiously upon the silent stockade, but were sent reeling back as soon as they had come near enough for the riflemen within to fire with absolute accuracy of aim. Then the second body, under Francis himself, charged, but with no better success. A pause followed, and another charge was made just before nightfall.

This time some of the savages succeeded in reaching the stockade and stopping up some of the port-holes. They cut down a part of the pickets too, and had their friends charged again at once, the fort would undoubtedly have been carried. As it was, Francis saw fit to draw off his men, for the time at least, and retire beyond the hill. What was now to be done? The attack had been repulsed, but it might be renewed at any moment. The Indians had suffered considerably, while the casualties within the fort were limited to the loss of one man and one boy. But the obstinate determination of Francis was well known, and it was certain that he had not finally abandoned his purpose of taking the little fort. He had already demonstrated his ability to carry the place, and it was, at the least, likely that he would come again within twenty-four hours, probably with a larger force, and should he do so, the little garrison was not in condition to repel his attack. To remain in the fort, therefore, was certain destruction; but the country was full of savages, and to attempt a march to Fort Glass, fifteen miles away, which was the nearest available place, the other forts being difficult to reach, was felt to be almost equally hazardous. A council was held, and it was finally determined that the perilous march to Fort Glass must be undertaken at all hazards. Accordingly, not long after nightfall the whole garrison, men, women and children, stealthily left the fort and silently crept away to the south.

Sam had seen the dog charge and the escape of the whites into the fort.

"What a fool I was!" he exclaimed, "not to stay where I was! We might have got in with the rest of them."

"Why can't we go to de fort now, or leastways, as soon as de Injuns goes away?" asked Joe.

"They ain't going away," said Sam. "They're going to storm the fort,—look, they're coming right here for a starting-point, and 'll be on top of us in a minute. Come!—don't make any noise, but follow me. Crawl on your hands and knees, and don't raise your heads. Look out for sticks. If you break one, the Indians 'll hear it."

"Mas' Sam—dey's Injuns ahead'n us an' a-comin right torge us too. Look dar!"

Sam looked, and saw a body of Indians just in front of him coming to reinforce the others. He and his friends were cut off between two bodies of savages.

"Lie down and be still," he whispered. "It's all we can do— and I'm to blame for it all!"

CHAPTER III

SAM'S LECTURE

The people of the fort made no search for Sam and his companions; not because they cared nothing for them, but simply because they believed them certainly dead. Mr. Hardwicke, himself, had seen Sam start with little Judie towards the fort, before the dog charge was made, and as neither the boys nor Judie had ever reached the gates, he had no doubt whatever that his three children were slain, as was Mrs. Phillips, the only other person who had failed to get inside the stockade. Mr. Hardwicke wished to go out in search of their bodies, but was overruled by his companions, who, knowing that the savages were still in the immediate vicinity, thought it simply a reckless and unnecessary risk, to go hunting for the bodies of their friends hundreds of yards away, and immediately in front of the place at which the Indians were last seen. The idea was abandoned, therefore, and the fort party marched away in the darkness of a cloudy night, towards Fort Glass. Leaving them to find their way if they can, let us return to Sam and his little band. Seeing the Indians coming towards them, they lay down in the high weeds. The savages hurrying forward to reinforce their friends, passed within a few feet of the young people, but did not see them. The storming of the fort then began, and after watching the evolutions of the Indians for some time, Sam said:

George Cary Eggleston

"We mustn't stay here. Those red skins are working around this way, and 'll find us. Crawl on your hands and knees, all of you, and follow me."

"Whar's ye gwine to, Mas' Sam?" asked Joe.

"*Sh, sh,*" said Judie. "Don't talk Joe, but do as Brother Sam tells you. Don't you know he always knows what's best? Besides, maybe he hasn't quite found out where he's going yet, himself."

But Joe was not as confident of Sam's genius for doing the right thing as Judie was, and so, after crawling for some distance, he again broke silence.

"Miss Judie."

"What do you want, Joe?"

"Does *you* know whar Mas' Sam's a-takin' us to, an' what he's gwine to do when he gits dar?"

"No, of course I don't."

"How you know den, dat he's doin' de bes' thing?"

But the conversation was terminated by a word from Sam, who said, in a whisper,

"Joe, I'll tell you *where we're going if you keep talking.*"

"Whar, Mas' Sam?"

"Into the hands of the Indians. Keep your mouth shut, if you don't want your hair lifted off your head."

As the black boy certainly did not want his hair cut Indian

fashion, he became silent at once.

When they had travelled in this way until they could no longer hear the yells of the Indians and the popping of guns at the fort, Sam called a halt. It was now nearly midnight.

"Here is a good place to spend the rest of the night," he said, "and we must be as still as we can. We can stay here till to-morrow night, and then we must try to get to Fort Glass. It's about twelve or thirteen miles from here."

"Le's go on now, Mas' Sam; I'se afear'd to stay here," said the black boy.

"We can't," said Sam. "I got scratched in the foot with a stray bullet, just as we went into the thicket there at the fort, and I can't walk. I am a little faint and must lie down."

At this little Judie, who fairly idolized Sam, and felt perfectly safe from Indians and everything else when he was with her, was disposed to set up a wail of sorrow and fright. If poor Sam were wounded, he might die, she thought, and the thought was too much for her.

Sam soothed her, however, and the poor, tired little girl was soon fast asleep in his arms.

"Bring some moss, boys," he said to his companions, "and make a bed for Judie here by this log."

When he had laid her down, he drew off his shoe and wrapped the wounded foot in some of the long gray moss which hangs in great festoons from the trees of that region. Joe, with the true negro genius for sleeping, was already snoring at the foot of a tree. Sam quietly called Tom to his side.

"Tom," said he, "my foot is bleeding pretty badly, and I can't see till morning to do anything for it. I have wrapped it up in moss, stuffing the softest parts into the wound, and that may stop it after a while. But I may not be able to travel to-morrow night, and if I can't you must leave me here and try to find your way to Fort Glass, with Judie. You must remember that her life will depend on you, and try to do your duty without flinching. Don't try to travel in the daytime. Go on to the south as fast as you can of nights, keeping in the woods and thickets, and as soon as you see a streak of gray in the sky find a good hiding-place and stop. You can get some corn and some sweet potatoes out of any field, but you must eat them raw, as it wont do to make a fire. Now go to sleep. I may be able to travel myself, but if I shouldn't, remember you are a brave man's son, and must do your duty as a Hardwicke should." And with that he shook the little fellow's hand.

After a time Tom, overcome by weariness, fell asleep, but Sam remained awake all night, trying to staunch the flow of blood from his foot. He knew that if he could go on with the others their chance of safety would be vastly greater than without him, and so he was disposed to leave no effort untried to be in a fit condition to travel the next night. When morning came Sam called Tom and Joe, and directed them to examine his wound, into which he could not see very well.

"Is the blood of a bright red, as it comes out, or a dark red?" he asked.

"Bright," they both said.

"Then it comes from an artery," he replied. "Are you sure it is bright red?"

The boys were not quite sure.

"Does it come in a steady stream or in spurts?" he asked.

"It spurts, and stops and spurts again," said Tom.

"It is an artery, then," said Sam. "Look and see if you can find the place it comes from."

The boys made a careful examination and at last found the artery, a small one, which was cut only about half way across.

"All right," said Sam. "If that's the case, I think I know how to stop the blood. Put your finger in, and *break the artery clear in two*".

"O Sam, then you'll bleed to death," said Tom.

"No I won't. Do as I tell you."

"Let me cut it, then. It wont hurt you so much."

"No, no, no," cried Sam, staying his hand. "Don't cut it. Tear it, I tell you, and be quick."

Tom tore it, and the blood stopped almost immediately. Sam then bound the foot up with strips of cloth torn from his clothing, and as he did so said:

"Now I'll tell you both all about this so that you'll know what to do another time. If you know only *what* to do, you may forget; but if you know *why*, you'll remember. The blood comes out from the heart to all parts of the body in arteries, and when it leaves the heart it is bright red, because it is clean and pure. Your heart is a sort of force-pump, and every time it beats it forces the blood all over you. The arteries fork and branch out in every direction, until they terminate in millions of little veins smaller than the finest hairs, and these running together make bigger veins, through which the blood is carried to the lungs. In the veins it flows steadily, because the *capillary* veins, the ones like hairs, are so small that the spurts can't be felt beyond them. The blood in the veins is thick and dark, because it has taken up all the impurities from the system; but when it gets to the lungs your breath takes up all these and carries them off, leaving the blood pure again for another round. Now the arteries are long elastic tubes, that is to say, they will stretch a little, and fly back again, if you pull them, and when one is cut nearly but not quite off, the contraction keeps it wide open. If it is cut or torn entirely in two, the end draws back, and nine times in ten, if the artery is a small one, the drawing back shuts the end up entirely and the blood stops. But it is better to tear it than to cut it, because when torn the edges are jagged and it shrivels up more. I don't quite understand why, myself, but that is what the surgical books say. When anybody is hurt and bleeding badly, the first thing to do is to find out whether it is an artery or a vein that's cut. If the blood is bright and comes out in spurts, it's an artery. If it is dark, and flows steadily, it's a vein. If it's an artery and isn't cut quite in two, tear it in two. If that don't stop it, you must make a knot in a handkerchief and then press your finger above the cut in different places till you find where the artery is by the blood stopping. Then put the knot on that place and tie the handkerchief around the limb. You can stop a vein in the same way and more easily, but if it's a vein you must tie the handkerchief so that the cut place will be between it and the heart. You see the blood comes from the heart in the arteries, and goes back towards the heart in the veins, and so to stop an artery you tie inside, and to stop a vein outside of the cut place."

I think it altogether probable that Master Sam would have gone into quite a lecture on anatomy and minor surgery, if little Judie had not waked up just then complaining of hunger. What he told the boys, however, is well worth remembering. He took little Judie on his lap and sent the two boys out to find a field of potatoes or corn. When they came back all four made a breakfast of raw sweet potatoes, drinking water which Tom brought in his wool hat from a creek not very far away. Sam grew stronger during the day, and at night the party set out on their way to Fort Glass. Sam's foot was not painful, but he was afraid of starting the blood again, and so he held it up, walking with a rude crutch which he had made during the day.

George Cary Eggleston

CHAPTER IV

SAM FINDS IT NECESSARY TO THINK

It was twelve miles from their first encampment to Fort Glass, and if Sam had been strong and well, and the way open, they might easily have made the journey before morning, by carrying little Judie a part of the way. As it was, they had to go through the thickest woods to avoid Indians, and must move cautiously all the time, as they could never know when they might stumble upon a party of savages around a camp-fire, or sleeping under a tree. Those of my readers who live in the far South know what thick woods are in that part of the country, but others may not. The trees grow as close together as they can, and the underbrush chokes up the space between them pretty effectually. Then the great vines of various kinds wind themselves in and out until in many places they literally stop the way so that a strong man with an axe could not go forward a hundred feet in a week. In other places the thick cane makes an equally impenetrable barrier, and Sam needed all his knowledge of the forest to enable him to work his way southward at night through such woods as those. The little party of wanderers sometimes found themselves apparently walled in in the pitchy darkness, with no possible way out but Sam's instinct, as he called it, which was simply his ability to remember the things he had learned, and to put two facts together to find out a third, always extricated them. Once they found themselves in a swamp, where the water was about eight inches deep. The underbrush, canes and vines made it impossible for them to see any great distance in any direction.

"Oh, I know we will never get out of here," whined poor little Judie, ready to sink down in the water.

"Yes we will, lady bird," said Sam cheerily. "What's the good of having a big brother if he can't take care of you? Tell me that, will you? Keep your courage up, little girl, I think I know where we are. Let me think."

"I know wha' we is. Mas' Sam," said Joe.

"Where, Joe," asked Sam, incredulously.

"We'se dun' los',—dat's wha' we is," replied Joe.

Sam laughed.

"I know more than that," said Tom, "I know *where* we're lost."

"Wha', Mas' Tom?" cried Joe, eagerly.

"In a swamp," said Tom.

"And I know what swamp," said Sam, "which is better still. This swamp is the low grounds of a little creek, and I've been in it before to-night. I don't know just which way to go to get out, because I don't know just what part of the swamp we're in. But if my foot was well I'd soon find out."

"How, Mas' Sam?"

"I'd climb that sweet gum and look for landmarks."

"Lan' marks? what's dem, Mas' Sam? will dey bite?"

"No, Joe, I mean I would look around and find something or other to steer by,—a house an open field or something."

"I kin climb, Mas' Sam," replied Joe, "an' I'll be up dat dar tree in less'n no time."

And up the tree he went as nimbly as any squirrel might. As he went up, Sam cautioned him to make no noise, and not to shout, but to look around carefully, and then to come down and tell what he had seen.

"I see a big openin'," said Joe, when he reached the ground again, "an' nigh de middle uv it dey's a big grove, wid a littler one jis' off to de left."

"Yes," said Sam, "I thought you'd see that. That's where Watkins's house stood: now which way is it?"

"Which-a-way's what, Mas' Sam?"

"The opening with the groves in it."

"I 'clar' I dunno, Mas' Sam."

It had not entered Joe's head to mark the direction, and so he had to climb the tree again. In going up and coming down, however, he wound around the tree two or three times and was no wiser when he returned to the ground than before he began his ascent.

"Look, Joe," said Sam. "Do you see that bright star through the trees?"

"De brightest one, Mas' Sam?"

"Yes."

"Yes, I sees it."

"Well, climb the tree, and when you get to the top, turn your face towards that star. Then see which way the opening is, and remember whether it is straight ahead of you, behind you, or to the right or left."

Joe went up the tree again and this time managed to bring down the information that when he looked at the star the opening was on his left.

With the knowledge of locality and direction thus gained, Sam was not long in finding his way to firm ground again, and as soon as he did so he selected a hiding-place for the day, as the morning was now at hand.

The next night they had fewer difficulties, the woods through which they had to pass being freer from undergrowth than those they had already traversed, and when the third morning broke they were within a mile or two of Fort Glass. Sam thought at first of pushing on at once to the fort, but, seeing "Indian sign" in the shape of some smouldering fires near a spring, he abandoned the undertaking until night should come again, and hid his little company in the woods. Something to eat was the one immediate necessity. They were all nearly famished, and neither corn nor sweet potatoes were to be found anywhere in the vicinity. Sam directed the boys to bring some rushes from the creek bottoms, and peeling these, he and his companions ate the pith, which is slightly succulent and in a small degree nourishing. Sam had learned this fact by accident while out hunting one day, and Sam took care never to forget anything which might be useful. Towards night, when the rushes failed to satisfy their hunger, Sam was puzzling himself over the problem of getting food, when Tom asked him if he knew the name of a

George Cary Eggleston

singular tree he had seen while out after rushes.

"It has the biggest leaves I ever saw," he said, "and they all grow right out of its top. Some of 'em are six feet long, and they've got folds in 'em. There ain't any limbs to the tree at all."

"Where did you see that?" asked Sam eagerly.

"Right over there, about a hundred yards."

"Good! It's palmetto. I didn't know there was one this far from the sea though. Here, take my big knife and you and Joe go and cut out as much as you can of the soft part just where the leaves come out. It's what they call palmetto cabbage, and it's very good to eat too, I can tell you."

The boys, after receiving minute instructions, went to the palmetto-tree and brought away several pounds of the terminal bud. On this the little company made a hearty meal, finding the "cabbage," as it is called, a well-flavored, juicy and tender kind of white vegetable substance, very nourishing and as palatable as cocoanut, which it closely resembles in flavor. Storing what was left in their pockets, they began to prepare for their night's journey to the fort, which they hoped to reach within an hour or two. They were just on the point of starting when a party of Indians, under Weatherford, the great half-breed chief, who was the life and soul of the war, rode across a neighboring field, and settled themselves for supper within a dozen yards of Sam's camp. The sky was overcast with clouds, and so night fell even more quickly than it usually does in Southern latitudes, where there is almost no twilight at all. Sam made his companions lie down at the approach of the savages, and as soon as it was fairly dark, the little party crept silently away. Before leaving, however, Sam had heard enough of the conversation between Weatherford and Peter McQueen, the other great half-breed warrior, to know that he could not reach the fort that night. The two half-breeds talked most of the time in English, and Sam learned that they had a large body of Indians in the vicinity, who were scouring the country around Fort Glass. Sam knew enough of Indian warfare to know that there would be numerous small parties of savage scouts lurking immediately around the fort day and night, for the purpose of picking off any daring whites who might venture outside the gates, and especially any messenger who might attempt to pass from that to any other fortress. He knew, therefore, that for some time to come it would be impossible to reach Fort Glass, and penetrating the woods for a considerable distance he stopped and sat down on a log, burying his face in his hands, and telling his companions not to speak to him, as he wanted to think.

CHAPTER V

SAM'S FORTRESS

Sam's companions kept perfectly still. Their reverence for Sam had grown with every foot of their travels, and their confidence in his ability to get out of any difficulty, and ultimately to accomplish his purposes in the face of any obstacle, was now quite unbounded. And so, when he told them it was impossible to reach the fort and that he wanted to think, they patiently awaited the results of his thinking, confident that he would presently hit upon precisely the right thing to do.

After a while he raised his head from his hands and said:

"Come on, we must get clear away from here before morning;" but he said not a word about where he was going. His course was now nearly south-east, and just as the day was breaking he stopped and said:

"There is the river at last. Now let's go to sleep."

They obeyed him unquestioningly, though they had not the faintest idea where they were or what river it was which he had seen a little way ahead. When Sam waked it was nearly noon, and he ate a little of the palmetto cabbage left in his pockets, while the others slept. His face was very pale, however, and he sat very still until his companions aroused themselves. Then he explained.

"When I found that we could not get to Fort Glass, the question was, where should we go? Fort Stoddart is probably surrounded by Indians too, and so the only thing to do was to make our way down through the Tensaw Country to Mobile; but that is about eighty or a hundred miles away, and the fact is I am a little sick from my wound. My foot and leg are all swelled up, and I've been having a fever, so that I can't travel much further. It seemed to me that the best thing to do, under the circumstances, was to find a good hiding-place where it will be easy to get something to eat, and to stay there till I get better, or something turns up, and so I thought of the Alabama River as the very best place, because mussels and things of that kind are better than sweet potatoes, and here we are; now the next thing is to find a hiding-place, and I think I know where one is. It has a spring by it, too, which is a good thing, for drinking this swamp and creek water will make us all sick. I was all through here on a camp-hunt once, and I remember a place on the other side of the river where two big hollow trees stand right together on top of a sort of bluff. About fifty yards further down the river there is a spring, just under the bluff. We must find the place if we can, to-night, and to do it we must first get across the river. It's so low now we can easily wade it, I think, and Judie can be pushed across on a log."

As soon as night fell the plan was put into execution. The river was extremely low at the time, and Sam was confident that by choosing a wide place for their crossing, they could wade the stream easily; but lest there might be a channel too deep for that, he fastened four logs together with grapevines, and putting Judie on this raft bade the two boys tow it over, telling them that if they should find the water too deep for wading at any point, they could easily support themselves by clinging to the logs. They had no difficulty, however, and were soon on the east bank of the stream. Sam's task was a much harder one. The current was very rapid and the bottom too soft for the easy use of his crutch, while his strength was almost gone. His spirit sustained him, however, and after a while he reached the shore. When all were landed, the search began for the hiding-place Sam had described. It proved to be more than a mile higher up the river, and when they found it, the day was breaking. The trees were not hollow, as Sam had supposed. The river bank in that place is in three terraces, and the two great trees stood almost alone on the second one of these. The sandy soil had been gradually washed out from under the great trunks, so that the trees proper began about fifteen feet from the ground, the space below being occupied by a great net-work of exposed roots, some of them a foot or two in thickness, and others varying in size all the way down to mere threads. The freshets which had washed the earth away from the roots, had piled a great mass of drift-wood against one side of them. Sam made a careful examination of the place, and then all went to work. The two boys so disposed some of the drift-wood as to make a sort of covered passage from the edge of the bank to the two trees whose roots were interlaced with each other. Sam cut away some of the roots with his jackknife so as to make an entrance, and once inside the circle of outer roots, he was not long in making a roomy hiding-place for the whole party, immediately under the great trees.

"We can enlarge our house with our knives whenever we choose," he said, "and if we stay here long enough, we must make Judie a room for herself under the other tree, with a passage leading from this into it."

Sam said this to avoid saying something which would have alarmed and distressed the others. In truth he knew himself to be really ill, and believed that he would be much worse before being any better. For this reason he knew they must have more room than the present hiding-place afforded, and it was his plan to cut another room under the other tree, with a very narrow passage between. "Then," thought he, "if the Indians find us here, as I am afraid they will, they will find only poor sick Sam here in the outer room, and won't think of hunting further." Sam thought he was going to die at any rate, and his only care now was to save the lives of the others. He had made them gather some mussels at the river, and some green corn in a neighboring field, and he now said to the two boys, "These things must be cooked. It will not do for you to eat them raw any longer. They aren't wholesome that way, and so I've been thinking of a plan for cooking them. The spring is down under the lower bluff, and a fire down there won't make much smoke above the upper banks. We must make one out of drift-wood, but we mustn't use any pine. That smokes too much. The fire must be made in the daytime, because at night it would be seen too far. You boys must do the cooking, while I keep a look-out for Indians, and if any come within sight you can both get in here before they discover you, or if they do see you, they can't find you after you run away from the fire, and they will look for you out in the woods somewhere. Nobody would think of looking here. Now let me tell you how to cook the things. I was at a 'clam bake' in New England once, and I know how to make these mussels and corn taste well. You must dig a sort of fireplace in the sand bank and build your fire in there. When it burns away until you have a good bank of coals, you must put down on them a layer of the corn, in the shuck, then a layer of mussels, then a layer of corn, and finally cover them all up with coals and hot ashes, and leave them there for an hour or two, when they will be cooked beautifully."

"But Mas' Sam," said Joe.

"Well, what is it, Joe?"

"How's we gwine to git de fire?"

"Well, how do you think, Joe?"

"I 'clare I dunno, Mas' Sam, 'thout you got some flints an' punk in your pockets."

"No, I have no flints and no punk, Joe, but I'm going to get you some fire when the sun gets straight overhead."

"Is you gwine to git it from de sun, Mas' Sam?"

"Yes."

"What wid, Mas' Sam?"

"With water, Joe."

"Wid water, Mas' Sam! You'se foolin'. How you gwine to git fire wid water, *I'd* like to know."

"Well, wait and see. I'm not fooling."

To tell the truth, Tom was quite as much at a loss as Joe was, to know how Sam could get fire with water; but his confidence in his "big brother," as he called Sam, was too perfect to admit of a doubt or a question. As for Judie, she would hardly have raised her eyebrows if Sam had burned water, or whittled it into dolls' heads before her eyes. She believed in Sam absolutely, and supposed, as a matter of course, that he knew everything and could do anything he liked. But Joe was not yet satisfied that water could be made to assist in the kindling of a fire. He said nothing more, however, but carefully watched all of Sam's preparations.

That young gentleman began by tearing a strip of cotton cloth from his shirt, and picking it to pieces. He then gathered from the drift-wood a number of dry sticks, and broke and split them up very fine.

"We must have a few splinters of light-wood," he said; "but after the fire is once started, we mustn't put any more pine on."

So saying, he split off a few splinters from a piece of rich heart-pine, which Southern people call "light-wood," because the negroes use it instead of lamps or candles.

"Come now," said Sam, "its nearly noon, and I think I can get fire for you. Go up on top of the drift-pile, Tom, and look out for Indians. If you don't see any we can all go down to the spring together long enough to start a fire. Then I must come back to Judie, and I'll keep a look-out for Indians while you and Joe get the corn on. When you get it on, come back here and wait until it has time to cook. Stop a minute, Tom. Let's understand each other. If the one on the look-out sees Indians, he must let the others know; but it won't do to holler. Let me see. Can you whistle like a kildee, Tom?"

"Yes, or like any other bird."

"Can you, Joe?"

"I reckon I *kin*, Mas' Sam," said Joe, who, to prove his powers straightway gave a shrill kildee whistle, which nearly deafened them all.

"There, that'll do, Joe. Well, let's understand then, that if anyone of us sees Indians, he must whistle like a kildee. If the Indians hear it they'll think nothing of it."

Tom went to the look-out, and seeing no savages anywhere, returned, and the whole party, little Judie excepted, proceeded to the spring. Sam then laid his sticks down in a pile, and taking out his watch removed the crystal. This he filled with clear water from the spring, and holding it over the cotton ravellings, moved it up and down until the sunlight, passing through it, gathered itself into a small bright spot on the cotton. Joe, eager to see, thrust his head over Sam's shoulder, and directly between the glass and the sun.

"Take your head away, Joe, or I'll have to draw the fire right through it," said Sam, laughing.

"Mercy, Mas' Sam, don't do dat. I'se 'feard o' your witches' ways, anyhow," said Joe, drawing back. The glass was again put in position and the spot of bright sunlight reappeared. Presently a little cloud of smoke rose, and a moment afterwards, the cotton was fairly afire. It was not difficult now to get the light-wood and dry sticks to blazing, and a good fire was soon secured.

"Now boys," said Sam, "I'll go back to the drift-pile and keep a look-out. If you hear the kildee call, run in as quickly as you can. When you get the corn and mussels on, and covered up, come back at once."

No Indians showing themselves anywhere in the neighborhood, the boys got their dinner on or rather *in* the fire, and then returned to the root cavern to await the completion of the cooking process. When they were all safely stowed away in their places, Tom gave voice to the curiosity with which he was almost bursting.

"Sam," he said, "how did you do that?"

"How did I do what, Tom?"

"How did you make the sun set the cotton on fire?"

"I don't know whether I can make you understand it or not," said Sam, "but I'll try. You know light always goes in straight lines, if left to itself, don't you?"

"No, I didn't know that!

"Yes you did, only you never thought of it. If you want to keep light out of your eyes, you always put your hand between them and the light, because you know the light goes straight and so will not go around your hand."

"Yes, that's true, and when I want to make a shadow anywhere, I put something right before the light."

"Certainly. Well, the rays of the sun all come to us straight, and side by side. They are pretty hot, but not hot enough to set fire to anything that way. But if you can gather a good many of these rays together and make them all shine on one little spot, they will set fire to whatever they fall on. Now a piece of glass or any other thing that you can see through easily,—that is, any *transparent* thing, lets the sunlight through it, and if it is flat on both sides, it doesn't change the directions of the rays. But if both sides are rounded out, or if one side is rounded out and the other side is flat, it turns all the rays a little, and brings them right together in a point not far from the glass. If the sides are hollowed *in* instead of bulging out, the rays scatter, and if one side bulges out and the other bulges in, as they do in a watch crystal, one side scatters and the other side collects the rays, and so it is the same as if the glass had been perfectly flat, one side undoes the other's work. Now I have no glass which bulges out on both sides, and none that bulges out on one side and is flat on the other, but my watch crystal bulges out on one side and in on the other. But when I filled it with water, the water being as clear as the glass, it made it flat on top and bulging underneath, and so it gathered the sun's rays together in the light spot you saw, and set fire to the cotton."

"Yes, but why did you have to wait till noon?" asked Tom.

"Because the glass must be held right across the rays of light,

George Cary Eggleston

and as I couldn't turn the crystal to either side without spilling the water, I had to use it at noon, when the sun was almost exactly overhead, and its rays came nearly straight down. If I had had a glass rounded out on both sides I could have got fire any time after the sun was well up in the sky. Now let me tell you what they call all these different kinds of glasses. One that is flat on one side and bulges out on the other is called a *convex lens*; if it bulges out on both sides it is a *double convex lens*; if it is hollowed in on one side and flat on the other it is a *concave lens*; if hollowed in on both sides we call it a *double concave lens*; and when it is hollowed in on one side and bulged out on the other, as any watch crystal does, it is a *concave convex lens*."

"Where did you learn all that, Sam?" asked Tom.

"I learned part of it with father's spectacles, and part out of a book father lent me when I asked him why I couldn't make the bright, hot spot with a pair of near-sighted glasses that I found in one of mother's old work boxes. You see, when people begin to get old, their eyes flatten a little, and so everything they look at seems to be shaved off. They see well enough at a distance, but can't see small things close to them."

"Is that the reason pa always looks over his spectacles when he looks at me?" asked Judie.

"Yes, little woman. He can't see to read without his glasses, but he can see you across the room without them, well enough. Well, to remedy this defect, old people wear spectacles with double convex lenses in them. But near-sighted people have exactly the opposite trouble. They can't see things except by bringing them near their eyes, because their eyes are not flat enough, and so their spectacles are made with double concave lenses. When I asked father about it, he gave me a book that explained it all, and that is where I learned the little I know about it."

"The *little*! I'd like to know what you call a good deal," said Tom. "I never saw anybody that knew half as much as you do."

"That is only because we live in a new country, Tom, where there are no very well educated people, and because you don't know how much there is to learn in the world. If these Indians ever get quiet, I hope to learn a good deal more every year than I know now. But it's time to see about our mussel bake. Run to the look-out, Tom, and then we can all go down and bring up the dinner."

CHAPTER VI

SURPRISED

The baked corn and mussels made a savory dish, or one which would have been savory enough but for the absence of salt. The boys knew well enough that salt was not to be had, however, and so they made a joke of its absence, and even pretended that they did not like their food salted at any time. Little Judie was so hungry that she cared very little whether food tasted well or not, provided it satisfied her appetite.

The rest and the more wholesome food seemed to restore Sam to something like his customary strength during the first ten days of his stay in the "root fortress," as he had named their singular dwelling. His wounded foot got better, though it was still far from well, and, better than all, his fever left him. As he regained strength he began to lay plans again. To stay where they were was well enough as a temporary device for escaping the savages, but Sam's main purpose now was to get the little people under his charge back to civilization somewhere, and then to do his part in the war between the Indians and whites. He must first find a way to get Tom and Judie and Joe into one of the forts or into some safe town, and how to do this was the problem. He was unwilling to take them away from their present pretty secure hiding-place until he could decide upon some definite plan offering a reasonable prospect of escape. If he could have known as much as we now know of the movements of the savages, he would have had little difficulty. The larger part of the Indians had left the peninsula now forming Clarke County, and crossed to the south-eastern shore of the Alabama river,—the side on which Sam's root fortress stood, and if he could have known this, he would have made an effort to cross the river again and reach Fort Glass. The chief difficulty in the way of this undertaking would have been that of crossing the river, which was now swollen by recent rains. He knew nothing about the matter, however, and as Fort Mims, the first point attacked by the savages, was on the south-east side of the river, he reasoned that having afterwards crossed to Clarke County the Indians would not again cross to the south-east side in any considerable force. In this, as we know, he was mistaken, and the error led him into some danger, as we shall see. Thinking the matter over, he decided that his first plan of a march down through the Tensaw Country to the neighborhood of Mobile would be the safest and best thing to undertake. He was unwilling, however, to begin it with his companions without making a preliminary reconnoissance. Accordingly he explained the plan to Tom and Joe, and said:

"I'm going to-night down towards old Fort Mims, to see if the country is pretty free from Indians, and to find out what I can about the chance of getting away from here. I'll leave you here with Judie, and you must be extra careful about exposing yourselves. You've corn and mussels and sweet potatoes enough already cooked, to last you a week, and I'll probably be back before that; if not you must eat them raw till I do come: it won't do to build a fire while I'm away." After giving minute directions for their guidance during his absence, Sam put a sweet potato in one pocket and an ear of corn in the other, and set out on his journey, walking with a stout stick, having discarded his crutch as no longer necessary. How far he walked that night, I am unable to say, his course being a very circuitous one. The moon rose full, soon after dark, and shone so brightly that Sam dared not cross the fields, but skirted around them keeping constantly in the woods and the edges of canebrakes. The next night and the next he continued his journey, though he found the country full of Indians. He saw their "sign" everywhere, and now and then saw some of the Indians themselves. The fourth evening found him so lame (his foot having swelled and become painful again) that he could not possibly go on. He had already gone far enough to discover that the country on that side of the river was too full of Indians for him to carry his little party safely through it, and so he determined to work his way back to the root fortress, and try the other side. Seeing a house in a field near by the place in which he had spent the day, he resolved to visit it for the purpose of bringing away any article he could find which might be useful to him in his effort to provide for his little band. In a grove near the house he found a horse,—a young and powerful animal, and as he feared his lameness would not permit him to reach his root fortress again on foot, he determined to ride the animal in spite of the fact that on horseback he would be in much greater danger of discovery by the Indians than on foot. The horse had a bridle on, and had evidently escaped, probably during a skirmish, from its white or red master.

Sam tied him in the grove, and went on to the house, which had been sacked and partially burned. Looking around in the moonlight, Sam discovered a hatchet, and, in the corner of what had once been a store-house, the remains of a barrel of salt. These were two valuable discoveries. The hatchet would be of great service to him not only in the root fortress but even more in forcing a pathway through the canebrakes when he should again cross the river and try to reach one of the forts. The salt he must have at any cost, and as he had no bag he made one by ripping off the sleeve of his coat and tying its ends with strips of bark. He had just filled it, and tied up the ends when, hearing a noise, he turned, and saw two Indians within six feet of him.

CHAPTER VII

CONFUSED

The two Indians who had startled Sam, were on the point of entering the old dwelling house, and seemingly were unaccompanied by any others. Sam happened fortunately to be standing in shadow, and they passed without seeing him. But what was he now to do? He was at the back of the house, and a high picket fence around the place made it impossible for him to escape by the front-way, towards which the savages had gone. Looking through the door-way, he saw that the pair had passed through the room nearest him and into the adjoining apartment. He knew that other Indians were in the neighborhood, and that a dozen of them might wander into the enclosure at any moment. Resolving upon a bold manoeuvre, he stepped lightly into the rear room of the house, and climbed up inside the wide mouthed chimney. Whether the Indians heard him or not he never knew, but at any rate he was none too soon in hiding, for he had hardly cleared the fireplace in his ascent when four or five savages came into the room and began to demolish the few articles of furniture left in the house. They had got whiskey somewhere, and having drank freely were even noisier than white men get under the influence of strong drink. They remained but a short time, when, setting fire again to the half-burned house, they left the place yelling as savages only can. Sam escaped as soon as he could from his uncomfortable quarters and

George Cary Eggleston

made his way to the grove. Mounting his horse he rode away in the direction of the root fortress, keeping in the woods as well as he could and taking every precaution to avoid coming suddenly upon savages.

As he rode only at night, the Indians' almost universal habit of building camp-fires wherever they stop for the night, helped him to avoid them. When morning came he sought a place deep in the forest, when he turned his horse loose to graze all day, while he slept at some distance from the animal, so that the noise of the beast's stamping and browsing might not lead to the discovery of his own whereabouts.

As the evening of the second day of his return came round, Sam found himself genuinely sick. His foot and leg were much inflamed, and the excitement of the preceding night, together with his continued exposure to the drenching dews of the Southern autumn, had brought back his fever with increased violence, and a very brief experiment convinced him that he could not go further that night. He mounted his horse, but had ridden less than a mile when he felt a giddiness coming over him and found it necessary to abandon the effort to ride that night. He could hardly see, and the pain in his head, neck, back and limbs was excruciating. He dismounted and threw himself down on the ground without taking the trouble even to separate himself from his horse. The truth is, Sam had what they call in South Carolina country fever, a high type of malarial fever, which stupefies and benumbs its victim almost as soon as it attacks him. The dews in the far South, especially in the fall, are so heavy that the water will drip and even stream off the foliage of the trees all night, and Sam had been drenched every night during both his journeys, having no fire by which to warm himself or dry his clothes. Even without this drenching the poisonous exhalations of the swamps and woods would doubtless have given him the fever, and as it was he had it very severely. He laid down again almost under his horse's feet and fell into a sort of stupor. He knew that his fever required treatment, and that it would rapidly sap his strength, and the thought came to him: What if he should die there and never get back to the tree fortress? He was too sick to care for himself, but the thought of little Judie haunted his dreams, and he was seized with a semi-delirious impulse to remount his horse and ride straight away to the hiding-place in which he had left her, regardless of Indians, and of everything else. He dreamed a dozen times that he was doing this, and finally, when morning came, he forgot all about the danger of travelling by daylight, and mounting his horse in a confused, half-delirious way, rode straight out of the woods towards the open country, which he had hitherto so carefully avoided.

George Cary Eggleston

CHAPTER VIII

WEATHERFORD

The fiercest and most conspicuous leader of the Indians in this war was William Weatherford, or the Red Eagle, as the Indians called him. He is commonly spoken of in history as a half-breed, but he was in reality almost a white man, with just enough of the Indian in his composition to add savage emotions to Scotch intellect and Scotch perseverance. His father was a Scotchman, and his mother a half-breed Indian Princess. He was brought up in the best civilization the border had, his father being wealthy. He became very rich himself, and, despite his savage instincts, which were always strong, his wealth, in land and slaves, made him a conservative. At first he favored a war with the whites, but a calmer afterthought led him to desire peace, and when he found that the tempest he had helped to stir up would not subside at his bidding, he began casting about for a way of escape. He was a man of unquestionable genius; a soldier of rare strategic ability; an orator of the truest sort, and his courage in danger was simply sublime. Such a man was likely to be of great value to the Indians in their approaching war, and when they began to suspect his loyalty to the nation, they watched him narrowly. Finding it impossible to postpone the war, and not wishing to sacrifice his fine property near the Holy Ground, he made a secret journey to the residence of his half brother David Tait and his brother

John Weatherford, who lived among what were known as the "peacefuls," namely, the Indians disposed to remain at peace with the whites in any event. His brothers, hearing his story, advised him to bring his negroes, horses and movable property generally, together with his family, to their plantations, and to remain there, inactive and neutral, during the struggle. When he returned to his residence for the purpose of doing this, however, he found that the hostile Indians had seized his family and his negroes as hostages, and, under the compulsion of their threat that they would kill his wife and children if he should dare to remain at peace, he joined in the war against the whites, becoming the fiercest of all the chieftains. He planned and led the assault upon Fort Mims, and was everywhere foremost in all the fighting. When the Creeks were utterly routed at the battle of the Holy Ground a month or so after the time of which I am writing, General Jackson issued a proclamation refusing terms of peace to the chiefs until Weatherford, whom he had determined to put to death, should be brought to him, alive or dead. Weatherford hearing of this, although he was safe beyond the borders and might have easily made his escape to Florida, as his comrade Peter McQueen did, rode straightway to Jackson's headquarters, where he said to the commander who had set a price upon his head:—

"I am Weatherford. I have come to ask peace for my people. I am in your power. Do with me as you please. I am a soldier. I have done the white people all the harm I could. I have fought them and fought them bravely. If I yet had an army I would fight and contend to the last. But I have none. My people are all gone. I can now do no more than weep over the misfortunes of my nation."

Jackson was so impressed with the sublime courage and the dignity of the man upon whose head he had set a price, that he treated him at once with chivalrous consideration. He told him that the only terms upon which the Indians could secure peace were unconditional submission and uniform good conduct; but "as for yourself," he said, "if you do not like the terms, no advantage shall be taken of your present surrender. You are at liberty to depart and resume hostilities when you please. But if you are taken then, your life shall pay the forfeit of your crimes."

Weatherford calmly folded his arms and replied; "I desire peace for no selfish reasons, but that my nation may be relieved from its sufferings; for independent of the other consequences of the war, my people's cattle are destroyed and their women and children destitute of provisions. I may well be addressed in such language now. There was a time when I had a choice and could have answered you. I have none now. Even hope has ended. Once I could animate my warriors to battle. But I cannot animate the dead. My warriors can no longer hear my voice. Their bones are at Talladega, Tallashatche, Emuckfaw and Tohopeka. I have not surrendered myself thoughtlessly. While there were chances of success I never left my post nor supplicated peace. But my people are gone, and I now ask peace for my nation and myself. On the miseries and misfortunes brought upon my country, I look back with the deepest sorrow, and wish to avert still greater calamities. If I had been left to contend with the Georgia army, I would have raised my corn on one bank of the river and fought them on the other. But your people have destroyed my nation. General Jackson, you are a brave man,—I am another. I do not fear to die. But I rely upon your generosity. You will exact no terms of a conquered and helpless people but those to which they should accede. Whatever they may be it would now be folly and madness to oppose them. If they are opposed, you shall find me among the sternest enforcers of obedience. Those who would still hold out can only be influenced by a mean spirit of revenge. To this they must not and shall not sacrifice the last remnant of their country. You have told us what we may do and be safe. Yours is a good talk, and my nation ought to listen to it. They *shall* listen to it."[1]

[Footnote 1: For these speeches of Weatherford's and for other historical details I am indebted to a valuable and interesting book, "Romantic Passages in South Western History," by A. B. Mull, Mobile, S. H. Goetzsl & Co. publishers, which is now, unfortunately out of print. The speeches are well authenticated I believe.]

Jackson was too generous and too brave a man to remain unmoved under such a speech from a man who thus placed his own life in jeopardy for the sake of his people. He bade the chieftain return home, and promised peace to his people, a promise faithfully kept to this day. All this however occurred nearly two months after the time of which I write, and it is introduced here merely by way of explaining the things which happened to Sam on the morning of the rash resumption of his journey.

This man Weatherford, the fiercest enemy the whites had, with a party of about twenty-five Indians, bivouacked, the night before, in the edge of the woods, and when Sam mounted his horse that morning the Indians were lying asleep immediately in his path as he rode blindly out of the thicket. The first intimation he had of their presence was a grunt from a big savage who lay almost under his horse's feet. Coming to himself in an instant, Sam took in the whole situation at a glance, and with the rapidity and precision which people who are accustomed to the dangers and difficulties of frontier life always acquire, he mentally weighed all the facts bearing upon the question of what to do, and decided. He saw before him the savages, rising from the ground at sight of him. He saw their horses browsing at some little distance from them. He saw a rifle, on which hung a powder-horn and a bullet-pouch, standing against a bush. He saw that he had already aroused the foe, and that he must stand a chase. His first impulse was to turn around and ride back, in the direction whence he had come; but in that direction lay the thicket through which he could not ride rapidly, and so if he should take that course, he would lose the advantage which he hoped to gain from the fleetness of his particularly good horse. Besides, in the thicket he must of course leave a trail easily followed. Just beyond the group of Indians he saw the open fields, and he made up his mind at once that he would push his horse into a run, dash right through the camp of the savages, pick up the convenient rifle if possible, and reaching the open country make all the speed he could. In this he knew he would have an advantage, inasmuch as he would get a good many hundred yards away before the savages could catch and mount their horses for the purpose of pursuing him, and he even hoped that they, seeing how far he was in advance of them, would abandon the idea of pursuit altogether. All this thinking, and weighing of chances, and deciding was the work of a single half second, and the plan, once formed, was executed instantly. Without pausing or turning he pushed his horse at a full run through the group of savages, receiving a glancing blow from a war club and dodging several others as he went. He succeeded in getting possession of the rifle which stood by the bush, and reached the field before a gun could be aimed at him. It was now his purpose to get so far ahead as to discourage pursuit, and with this object in view he continued to urge his horse forward at his best speed. This hope was a vain one, as he soon discovered. The Indians, infuriated by his boldness, mounted their horses and gave chase immediately. Sam had an excellent habit, as we know, of keeping his wits about him, and of preparing carefully for difficulties likely to come. The first thing to be done was to escape, if possible, and so he continued to press his high-spirited colt forward, while he debated the probabilities of being overtaken, and discussed with himself the resources at his command if the savages should come up with him. He was armed now, at any rate, and if running should prove of no avail, he could and would sell his life very dearly. Indeed the possession of the rifle roused all the spirit of battle there was in him, and great as the odds were against him, he was sorely tempted to pause long enough to shoot once at least. He remembered Tom and Judie and Joe, however, and their dependence upon him for guidance and protection, and for their sake more than for his own, suppressed the impulse and continued his flight. The Indians were nearly half a mile behind him, and, as nearly as he could tell, were not gaining upon him very rapidly. His colt seemed equal to a long continued race, and as yet showed no sign of faltering or fatigue. The question had now resolved itself, Sam thought, into one of endurance. How long the Indians would continue a pursuit in which he had the advantage of half a mile the start, he had no way of determining, but that his horse's endurance was as great at least as their perseverance, he had every reason to hope.

Just as he had comforted himself with this thought, a new danger assailed him. One of the Indians, it seemed, taking advantage of a minute knowledge of the country, had saved a considerable distance by riding through a strip of woods and cutting off an angle. When Sam first caught sight of him, coming out of the woods, the savage was within a dozen yards of him, and evidently gaining upon him at every step. Sam's horse was a fleet one, but that of the Indian was apparently a thoroughbred, whose speed remained nearly as great after a mile's run as at the start. Knowing the Indians' skill in shooting while riding at full speed, Sam leaned as far as he could to one side, so that as little as possible of his person should be exposed to his pursuer's aim. He continued to press his horse too, but the savage gained steadily. Finding at last that he must shortly be overtaken, Sam resolved upon a bold manoeuvre, by which to kill his foremost pursuer. Seizing the hatchet he had brought away from the house, he suddenly stopped his horse, and, as the Indian came along-side, aimed a savage blow at his head.

"Don't you know me, Sam?" said the Indian in good English,

George Cary Eggleston

dodging the blow. "I'm Weatherford. If I'd wanted to kill you I might have done so a dozen times in the last five minutes. You know I don't want to kill *you*, though you're the only white man on earth I'd let go. But the others will make an end of you if they catch you. Ride on and I'll chase you. Turn to the left there and ride to the bluff. I'll follow you. There's a gully through the top. Ride down it as far as you can and jump your horse over the cliff. It's nearly fifty feet high, and may kill you, but it's the only way. The other warriors are coming up and they'll kill you sure if you don't jump. Jump, and I'll tell 'em I chased you over."

Sam knew Weatherford well, and he knew why the blood-thirsty chief wished to spare him if he could, for Sam had rescued Weatherford once from an imminent peril at great risk to himself, though the story is too long to be told here. Whether or not there is nobleness enough in the Indian character to make the savage remember a benefit received, I am sure I cannot say, but Weatherford was *three-fourths white*, and with all his ferocity in war, history credits him with more than one generous impulse like that by which Sam was now profiting. The two rode on, Weatherford pretending to be in hot pursuit, shooting occasionally and yelling at every leap of his horse. The bluff towards which they rode was probably a hundred feet high, and was washed at its base by a deep but sluggish creek, on the other side of which lay a densely wooded swamp. Through the top of the bluff, however, was a sort of fissure or ravine washed by the flow of water during the rainy season, and where it terminated the height of its mouth above the stream was not more than forty or fifty feet. Down this gully Sam rode furiously, so that his horse might not be able to refuse the leap, which was a frightful one. Coming to the edge of the precipice with headlong speed, the animal could not draw back but plunged over with Sam sitting bolt upright on his back. Riding back to the top of the bank Weatherford met his warriors.

"Where is he?" asked the foremost.

"His *body* is down there in the creek. I drove him over the precipice," said the chief with well-feigned delight.[2]

[Footnote 2: This incident of the leap over the precipice is strictly historical, else I should never have ventured to print it here. Weatherford himself, on the 23d of December, 1813, after the battle of Tohopeka, escaped a body of dragoons in a precisely similar manner. A still more remarkable leap was that of Major Samuel McCullock, on the 2d of September 1777, over a precipice fully 300 feet high near Wheeling, West Virginia. He jumped over on horseback, thinking such a death preferable to savage torture, but singularly enough, both he and his horse escaped unhurt.]

His purpose evidently, was to satisfy the warriors that Sam was certainly killed, so that they might pursue him no further. Whether he was yet alive or not, Weatherford himself had no means of knowing. The last he had seen of him was as he went over the precipice, sitting bolt upright on his horse, grasping his rifle and looking straight ahead. He heard a splash in the water below, after which everything was still.

CHAPTER IX

WEARY WAITING

The days seemed very long to Tom and Joe and little Judie after Sam left on his journey. They had nothing to do but to sit still in their corners among the roots all day, and time always drags very slowly when people are doing nothing. Their provisions, as we know, were already cooked,— enough of them at least, to last a week, and before Sam left he had made them bring more than a bushel of sweet potatoes and all the corn they could find which was still soft enough to eat, and store it away for use if his return should be delayed in any way. The result was that their legs got no stretching, and they became moody, dispirited and unhappy before the second day of Sam's absence had come to an end. They found doing nothing the hardest and the dullest work they ever had done in their lives. Joe managed to sleep most of the time, but Tom was nervous, and poor little Judie, without Sam to depend upon, grew low-spirited and began to fear all sorts of evil things. Finally Sam's week was up and Sam had not appeared. The little people were now fairly frightened. What had become of him? they wondered. Had he fallen into the hands of the Indians? And if so, what were they to do now? They never before known how dependent they were upon him. Even during his absence they had been regulating their lives by his minute instructions, and depending upon him for guidance after he should return.

But what if he should never return? And why hadn't he come already? These thoughts were too much for them. Judie sat in her corner brooding over her trouble, and crying a little now and then. Joe was simply frightened, and his eyes grew bigger and rounder than ever. Tom was sustained in part by the thought that the burden of responsibility was now on him, and so he suppressed all manifestations of uneasiness, as well as he could, and gave himself up to the duty of studying the situation, calculating his resources and trying to decide what was the best thing to be done if Sam should not come back at all. He hit upon several excellent ideas, but made up his mind that before trying to put any of them into practice he would wait at least a fortnight longer for Sam's return. Their stock of provisions, eaten raw, would last much longer than that, and the fields were full of sweet potatoes, wherefore he wisely thought it best not to lose any chance of having Sam to do the thinking and planning. He was so anxious for his brother's return that he spent the greater part of his time on the drift-pile where he had built himself a little observatory, so arranged that he could see in every direction without the possibility of being seen in his turn.

Sitting there in his look-out, watching for Sam, he had time to think of many things. His thinking was not always wise, as a matter of course, but for a boy of his age it did very well, certainly, and one day he hit upon a really valuable idea.

The way it came about was this. He fell into a reverie, and remembered the happy old days at home, and one day in particular, when he was busy all day making a little wagon in which to give Judie a ride, and he remembered how very short that day seemed, although it was in June. Just then it popped into his head to think that there was a reason for everything, and that that day had seemed so short only because he had been very busy as its hours went by. If he had known what "generalization" means, he would have generalized this truth as follows:—

George Cary Eggleston

"Time passes rapidly with busy people." He did nothing of the kind, however. He only thought.

"If poor little Judie had something to keep her busy all the time, she wouldn't be so miserable."

And so he cudgelled his brains to invent some plan or other by which to set Judie at work and keep her at it all the time.

When he returned to the fortress towards night, he said to the little woman; "Judie, I reckon poor Sam's foot is troubling him again, and that's the reason he hasn't got back yet. He'll work along slowly and get here after a while, but I'm afraid he'll be dreadfully tired and sick when he comes. We must have a good soft bed ready for him so that he can get a good rest."

To this Judie assented, though in her heart she feared she should never see Sam again, as indeed Tom did too, though neither would admit the fact to the other.

"Now I've been thinking," said Tom, "that it wont do, if he comes back half sick, to let him lie on green moss with all the outside on. Let me show you."

And taking a strand of the long moss he scraped the greenish gray outside off, leaving a black strand like a horse hair.

"There," he said, "Sam told me once that it's the soft outside part that holds water, while the inside is dry almost always. Now why can't we scrape the outside off of a great deal of moss and have the dry inside ready for Sam to sleep on when he comes back? It'll surprise him and he'll be glad too. He never cared for himself much, but he'll be glad to see that we care for him."

The plan pleased little Judie wonderfully well. She was

always delighted to do anything for Sam, and now that she was uneasy about him, and kept thinking of him as dead or dying or sick somewhere, and could hardly keep her tears back, nothing could have pleased her so well as to work for his comfort. Tom and Joe went out after dark, and brought in a large lot of moss, and the next morning all went to work, Judie made very little progress with her scraping, but she kept steadily at it, and it served its purpose in making her less miserable than before. The days passed more rapidly to Tom and Joe, too, and the whole party grew more cheerful under the influence of work. It was now ten days, however, since Sam had gone away, and his non-appearance was really alarming. When work stopped for the night, the thought of Sam was uppermost in the minds of all three, and for the first time they talked freely of the matter.

Tom was disposed to cheer himself by cheering the others, and so he explained:

"It's about forty-five miles to where Fort Mims stood, so Sam told me, and he said he might go nearly that far, if he didn't see Indians. If he went only thirty-five miles it would take him four or five nights; say five nights, and five more to come back would make ten. But may be his foot got sore, or Indians got in the way, and so it has taken him longer than he thought. I don't think we ought to be uneasy even if he should stay two weeks in all."

That was all very well as a theory, and true enough too, but Tom was uneasy, nevertheless, and so were Joe and Judie. The worst of it was that none of them could hide the fact. The eleventh day came, and with it came an excitement. Tom was the first to wake, and without waiting for the others, he proceeded to make his breakfast off an ear of raw corn, which was almost hard enough to grind, and altogether too hard to be eaten as green corn at any well-regulated table. Tom ate it, however, having nothing better, and when

Judie waked he offered her a softer ear, which he had carefully selected and laid aside. Judie tried but couldn't eat it. She was faint and almost sick, and found it impossible to swallow the raw corn.

"Poor little sister," said Tom. "If I had any fire I'd roast a potato for you to-day anyhow, but the fire's all out and I can't."

"Mas' Tom!" said Joe, "I'll tell you what! I dun see a heap o' fox grapes down dar by de creek, an' I'se gwine to git some for Miss Judie quicker'n you kin count ten." And so saying Joe ran first to the look-out, to make a preliminary reconnoissance. The boys rarely ever left the trees during the daytime, and when they did so they were careful first to satisfy themselves that there were no savages in the neighborhood. The creek, of which Joe spoke, emptied into the river a short distance above the root fortress, and, along its banks was a dense mass of undergrowth, which skirted the river below, all the way to the drift-pile. Joe had seen the grapes from the look-out, and had planned an excursion after them. He could follow the river bank to the creek, keeping in the bushes and moving cautiously, and if any Indians should appear he could retreat in the same way, without discovery. Tired of raw corn and sweet potatoes, the grapes had tempted him sorely, and it only needed Judie's longing for a change of diet to induce him, to make this foraging expedition.

CHAPTER X

FIGHTING FIRE

Before proceeding to relate the incidents which follows, it is necessary to explain a little more fully the arrangement of the root fortress and the drift-pile. The two trees, which were enormous ones, had originally grown as close together as they could, and their roots had interlaced beneath the soil. The sand in which they grew having been gradually washed away, their great masses of roots were exposed for about fifteen feet below the original level of the soil and as they spread out they made two circles (one running a foot or two into the other), of about twelve or fifteen feet in diameter. Inside of this circle of great roots, the roots were mostly small, and the boys had cut them away with their knives, leaving just enough of them to stop up all the holes and obscure the view from without. The drift-pile, or hammock, as it is sometimes called at the South, had been years in forming, being drift-wood which had floated down the river during winter and spring freshets, and as it had lodged against the trees it lay only on their upper side, where it was piled up into a perpendicular wall nearly twenty feet high. Thence it stretched away up the river for a hundred yards or more. Now the only entrance big enough to admit a person into the root fortress was on the side next to the drift, and it opened only into an alley-way which the boys had partly found and partly made through the drift. This alley-way led past several little aisles running out to the right and left for a dozen yards or so,—aisles formed by the irregular piling of the logs on top of each other. In the fortress there were a dozen places at least, where the big roots were sufficiently wide apart to admit a grown man easily, but the boys had left the smaller roots which covered these gaps undisturbed, and cut only the one entrance. After cutting that on the side next the hammock, they had moved some of the drift so as to close up the sides of the entrance and make it open only into the alley-way. All this had been done under Sam's supervision, and as a result of his prudence and fore thought.

Joe had been gone nearly half an hour when he burst suddenly into the chamber in which the others were. His hands were full of the wild grapes, but of those he was evidently not thinking. His face was of that peculiar hue which black faces assume when if they were white faces they would grow pale; and his lips, usually red, were of an ashy brown. His eyes were of the shape of saucers, and seemed not much smaller. He gasped for breath in an alarming way, and Tom saw that the poor fellow was frightened almost out of his wits.

"What's the matter Joe? Tell me quick," said the younger boy.

"O Mas' Tom, we'se dun surrounded. I was jest a-gittin' de grapes when I seed a'most a thousand Injuns a-comin',' an' I dun run my life a'most out a-gittin' here. Dey did not see me, but I seed dem, an' I tell you dey's de biggest Injuns you ever did see. I 'clar dey's mos' as tall as trees."

"How many of 'em are there, Joe?" asked Tom standing up.

"I couldn't count 'em e'zactly, Mas' Tom, but I reckon dey's not less'n a thousand of 'em,—maybe two thousan' for all I know."

"Where are they, and what were they doing?" asked Tom; but before Joe could answer, the voices of the Indians themselves indicated their whereabouts, and Tom discerned that they were disagreeably close to his elbow.

Seeking a place in which to cook their breakfast the savages had selected the corner formed by the root fortress and the drift-pile as a proper place for a fire, and were now breaking up sticks with which to start one. They were just outside the fortress, and either of the boys could have touched them by pushing his arm out between the roots. Tom motioned the others to keep absolutely silent, and going a little way into the hammock, through the passage way he managed to find a place from which he could see the intruders. He soon discovered that Joe's account of them was slightly exaggerated in two important particulars. They were only ordinary Indians, neither larger nor smaller than grown Indians usually are, and instead of a thousand there were but three of them in all.

But three fully grown Indians were enough to justify a good deal of apprehension, and if they should discover the party in the tree, Tom knew very well they would make very short work of their destruction. He crept back to the tree therefore and again cautioned Joe and Judie, in a whisper, not to speak or make any other noise. Then he returned to his place of observation and watched the Indians. They soon made a crackling fire and proceeded to broil some game they had killed, this and the eating which followed occupied perhaps an hour, during which Tom made frequent journeys to the little room, nominally for the purpose of cautioning the others to keep still, but really to work off some portion of his uneasiness, which was growing with every moment. He was terrified at first upon general principles, as any other boy of eleven years old would have been. Then he was afraid that the Indians would by some accident, lean something against the curtain of small roots between two other big trees, and that the curtain might not be strong enough to support it, in which event their hiding-place would be discovered at once. He was afraid, too, that some slight noise inside the fortress might catch the uncommonly quick ears of the Indians.

All these were dangers well worth considering; but now a new, and much greater danger began to show itself. The drift was largely composed of light wood, and from his hiding-place Tom could see that the fire built by the trees had communicated itself to the hammock, and that the flames were rapidly spreading. The danger now was that the fire would burn into the alley-way and so cut off retreat from the fortress, and if so those inside would be burned alive. Quitting his place of observation therefore, he established himself as a sentry in the alley-way, having determined, if the fire should approach the passage, to take Joe and Judie out of the fortress and into one of the aisles near the farther edge of the drift-pile. Having begun to plan he saw all the possibilities of the case and tried to provide for all. He knew that if the wind should drive the flames into the drift the whole pile would be destroyed in a very brief time, but in that case, he reasoned, the black smoke of the resinous pine would make it impossible for the Indians to see very far in that direction, and so he resolved, if the worst came, to lead his companions out of the upper end of the hammock, into the bushes and so escape to the creek, where he hoped to find a hiding-place of some sort. He had got this far in his planning when he heard Judie cough, and stepping quickly into the room found it full of smoke. Seeing that to stay there was to suffocate, he beckoned his companions to follow, and stepping lightly they passed down the alley-way and sat down in one of the aisles, behind a great sycamore log which ran across the pile. Peeping over this log Tom saw the three Indians shoulder their guns and walk away. He ran at once to the look-out, and though the smoke almost blinded him he observed all their movements. He wanted them away speedily, so that he and Joe might extinguish the fire if that were still possible, and as every minute served to increase the difficulty and lessen the chances of doing so, the loitering of the savages seemed interminable. They stopped first to drink at the spring. Then they amused themselves by throwing sticks, and pebbles and shells at a turtle which was sunning himself on a log in the stream. Then they stopped to examine the track of a turkey or of some animal, in the sand, and it really seemed to Tom that they did not mean to go away at all.

All things have an end, however, and even the stay of disagreeable visitors cannot last always. The three savages finally disappeared a mile down the river, and Tom, after scanning the surrounding country and satisfying himself that there were no others in the immediate neighborhood, hurried to the place where Joe and Judie were hidden.

"They've gone at least," he said, "and now Joe, we must put this fire out, if we can. Judie, you stay here, and if you find the smoke bothers you, go further down the alley that way. Don't try to stay if the smoke comes."

How to stop the fire was the problem. Fortunately there was very little wind, and what there was blew chiefly from up the river. The flames had spread over a considerable space, however, and the boys had hardly anything with which to work.

They carried water in their hats from the river, which was only a few yards away, now that it had risen to the bottom of the second bank. This was altogether too slow a way of working, however, and the fire was visibly gaining on the boys. But, slow as this process was, it served to teach Tom a lesson or rather to remind him of one he had learned and forgotten. He found that a hatful of water thrown on the bottom of the fire did more good than two hatfuls thrown on top, and he remembered that when the soot in the chimney at home caught fire once, his father would not allow anybody to pour water down the chimney, but stood himself by the fireplace throwing a little water, not up the chimney but, on the blazing fire below. This water, turned into steam, went up the chimney and soon extinguished the fire there. In the same way Tom now discovered that when he threw a hatful of water on a burning log at the bottom of the pile it had a perceptible effect all the way to the top. Thinking of the chimney fire he remembered also that his father had said at the time that a plank laid over the top of a burning chimney, or a screen fastened over the fireplace would stop the burning of the soot by stopping the air, and so smothering the fire. This suggested a new plan of operations for present use. The long gray moss grew in great abundance all around the place, and gathering this he dipped it in the river and then threw it on top of the fire. A bunch of the moss held greatly more water than his hat, and it served also to smother the fire. He and Joe repeated the operation, putting some of the moss on top and some against the sides of the burning pile of timber. The steam from these perceptibly checked the burning, and an hour's work covered the fire almost entirely up, so far at least as the exposed side of the drift-pile was concerned. But just as they were disposed to congratulate themselves upon their success in subduing the flames, they discovered that while they had been smothering the fire on one side it had been burning freely further in. The openness of the hammock gave free access to the air from the other side, and just beyond the line of moss they saw a blaze licking its tongue out from below. They were tired out, already, and this added discouragement to weariness. Little Judie, although the boys had urged her to remain quiet, had been hard at work bringing moss to them, insisting upon her right to work as well as they. She had discovered too that the sand, just below the surface was wet, and that this served almost as good a purpose as the moss itself when thrown on the fire. The poor little girl was utterly tired out at last, however, and when the fire seemed to be subsiding, she had yielded to Tom's entreaties, and going into the drift-pile had laid down to rest. Now that all their work promised to accomplish nothing, the boys were vexed with themselves for having permitted the frail little girl to wear herself out in so fruitless a task. This, with their disappointment, served to make them utterly wretched.

CHAPTER XI

IN THE WILDERNESS

When Sam went over the cliff, he thought of poor little Judie, and Tom and Joe, and, for their sake more than his own, took every precaution which might give him an additional chance of life. He knew that he should fall into the creek, and that the blow, when he struck the water, would be a very severe one. If he could keep his horse under him all the way, however, the animal and not he would be the chief sufferer. Fearing that the horse would hesitate at the cliff, blunder, and throw him a somersault, perhaps falling on him, he held the beast's head high and urged him forward at full speed, and so, as we have seen, the horse's back was almost level as he leaped from the top of the bank. Sam had no saddle or stirrups in which to become entangled, and as the horse struck the water fairly, the blow was not nearly so severe a shock to the boy as he had expected. Both went under the water, but rising again in a moment Sam slid off the animal's back, to give the poor fellow a better chance of escape by swimming. Striking out boldly Sam reached the bank and crawling up looked for his horse. The poor beast was evidently too severely hurt to swim with ease, and so he drifted away, Sam running along the bank, calling and encouraging him. He struck the shore at last, and Sam examining him found that while he was stunned and bruised no serious damage had been done.

"Poor fellow," he said, stroking the colt's head, "you cannot serve me any further in this swamp, but you saved my life and I'm glad you're not killed anyhow."

Then taking the bridle off, he turned the horse loose, to graze and browse at will in the dense growth of the swamp.

Sam was feverish still, and very weak, but his anxiety to reach the root fortress again was an overmastering impulse. He had lost his bearings in the mad chase, and the sky was so overcast that he could make no use of the sun as a guide. He knew that his course lay nearly northward, and it was his purpose to travel only at night, as before; but unless he could get out of the swamp during the day, and ascertain in what direction he must travel, he could not go on during the night at all. If it should clear off by evening, the pole star would show him his way, but there was no promise of a clearing away. He must find the course during the day, and he set about it at once, after examining his salt bag which he had put around his body, under his shirt, on the night on which he got it. The salt was saturated with water, and Sam's first impulse was to wring it out; but it occurred to him that the water he should squeeze out of it would be salt water, or in other words, that some of the salt would come away with the water and be lost. If he let it dry gradually, however, all the salt would remain, and he determined to let it dry, carrying it, with that in view, over his shoulder. How to find out which way was north was the question, and it puzzled him sorely. He knew the general course of all the creeks in that part of the country, but as they wind about in every direction it was impossible to get any information out of the one he was near. It was his habit, when he wanted to solve any difficult problem, to sit down and think of it in all its bearings, and a very excellent habit that is too. Nearly half our blunders, all through life, might be avoided if we would think carefully before acting; and nearly half the useful things we know, have been found out simply by somebody's thinking. Sam sat down on a log and said to himself;—

"Now if there is anything in the woods which always or nearly always points in any one direction, I can find it by looking. Then I can find out which way it points, by remembering how the woods look around home, where I know the points of the compass."

This was an excellent beginning, and Sam straightway began looking for something which should guide him. A patch of sunflowers grew by the creek, and he had heard that they always turn their heads to the sun, but upon examining them, he found some of them turned one way and some another, so that they were of no use whatever. Presently he observed some beautiful green moss growing at the root and for a good many feet up the trunk of a tree, and looking around he saw that the moss at the roots of all the trees grew only or chiefly on one side, and that the covered side was the same with all of them. Here was a uniform habit of vegetation, and Sam knew enough to know that such a habit was not likely to be confined to one particular locality. He began thinking of the woods around home, and especially of a clump of trees in the yard at his father's house, the moss-covered roots of which were Judie's favorite playing place. This moss, he remembered, was nearly all on the north side of the trees, whose southern roots were bare. All the other mossy trees he could remember taught the same lesson, namely, that the green moss which grows around the bases of trees, grows chiefly on the north side. He had no doubt that the law was a general, if not a universal one, and as the mossy trees were very numerous, he had a guide easily followed. Striking out northwardly, therefore, he travelled several miles before stopping, coming then to a suitable resting-place he lay down to gather strength for the night's journey. When night came, however, it had been raining for some hours, and in addition to the darkness of a rainy night in a swamp, Sam found the soft alluvial soil so saturated with water that he sank almost to his knees at every step. Finding it impossible to go on he stopped again on the highest and dryest piece of ground he could find, and prepared to spend the night there. Cutting down a number of thick-leaved bushes he arranged them against a fallen tree, as a shelter.

He had been lying down but a short time when he discovered that pretty nearly all the rain that fell on his bush roof found its way through in great drops from the leaves. It then occurred to him that he had erred in placing the bushes with their tops up. This indeed, made them mere catchers and conductors of water to the space they covered. Turning them, so that their drooping leaves pointed downward, he was not long in making a really comfortable shelter, through which very little water could find its way.

Towards morning he waked and found himself lying in water. He could see nothing in the darkness, but supposed that the rain had in some way made a pool where he was lying. On coming out from his tent, however, he found matters much worse than he had thought. In whatever direction he looked he could see nothing but water, and he knew what the trouble was. The rain had been very heavy all along the creek, and the stream having very little fall had spread out over the whole surface of the swamp. There was nothing to do except wait for daylight, and he climbed upon the trunk of the fallen tree to get out of the water while he waited. The rain had ceased to fall, and he had therefore no reason to fear any great increase in the depth of the surrounding water.

When morning came, Sam found that he was not the only occupant of the fallen tree. A fine large opossum had taken refuge in one of the upper branches, and Sam used his rifle to good purpose in bringing him down. He was still suffering somewhat from the fever, though the excitement of his recent ride had done much to relieve him, as anything which occupies one's mind is apt to do in fevers of that sort, but he was nevertheless extremely hungry, not having tasted food of any kind for nearly two days, and having previously lived for a long time, as we know, upon an insufficient and not very wholesome diet. He was delighted therefore to get a fat young opossum for breakfast. The next thing was to cook it. Sam was in no danger here from Indians, who were not likely to be in such a swamp at any time, and were certainly not then, when the swamp was full of water. He had no objection therefore to a fire, but where and how to build one he was at some loss to determine. Looking carefully around he discovered that in falling the great sycamore tree on which he stood had thrown up a large mound of earth at its roots, as big trees in blowing down nearly always do. This mound was well above the water, even at its base, and here Sam determined to roast his opossum. He first dug a hole in the ground, making it about two feet long, one foot wide and eighteen inches deep. This was to be his fireplace and oven. He next collected dry bark from the under side of the fallen tree, and by breaking off its dead and well-seasoned limbs secured several large armfuls of wood. Then taking from his leathern bullet-pouch a piece of greased rag, kept there to wrap bullets in before ramming them in the barrel, he placed it in the "pan" of his rifle. Does the reader know what the "pan" of a rifle is? If not he knows nothing of flintlock guns, and I must explain. Before the invention of percussion caps, guns were provided with a little groove-shaped trough by the side of the powder chamber. From this "pan" as it was called, a little hole led into the charge. Over the pan fitted a piece of steel on a hinge, so that it could be opened and shut at pleasure. This piece of steel, after covering the pan, extended diagonally upward, and its surface was roughened like the face of a file. When the rifleman had loaded his gun he opened the pan, poured in a little powder and closed it again. In the hammer was a piece of flint, and when the trigger was pulled the flint came down with great force into the pan, scraping the roughened steel as it came, and raising the pan cover on its hinge. It thus deposited a shower of sparks in the pan, set fire to the powder there and through it to the charge in the gun.

Sam's object was merely to get fire, however,—not to discharge his rifle,—wherefore, without reloading it, after shooting the opossum, he merely filled the pan with powder, placed the greasy rag in it, and cocking the gun pulled the trigger. In a moment the rag was burning, and before many minutes had passed, Sam had a good fire burning in and over the hole he had dug. He then skinned and dressed the opossum, stopping now and then to replenish the fire and to throw all the live coals into the hole as they formed. Within an hour the hole was full of burning coals, and hot enough, Sam thought, for his purpose. He cut a number of green twigs and collected a quantity of the long gray moss. He then removed all the fire from the hole, the sides and bottom of which were almost red hot, and passing a twig through the opossum, lowered it to the middle of the hole, where the twig rested on ledges provided for that purpose. This brought the dressed animal into the centre of the hole, without permitting it to touch either the sides or the bottom. He then laid twigs across the top of the hole, covered them with moss, and threw nearly a foot of loose earth over the moss. The sides and bottom of the hole, as I have said, were very hot, and Sam's plan was to keep the heat in until it should roast the meat thoroughly. That his plan was a good one, I know from experience, having roasted more than one turkey in that way. It is, in fact, the very best way in which meat of any kind can possibly be roasted at all, as it lets none of the flavor escape in the form of gases.

Sam waited patiently for an hour, when, opening his earth oven, he found his opossum cooked to a rich, crisp brown. He ate a heartier and more wholesome breakfast that morning than he had eaten for weeks, and felt afterwards altogether better and stronger than before. The breakfast would have been an excellent one at any time, as the flesh of the opossum tastes almost exactly like that of a suckling pig, but it was doubly good to the poor half-famished boy. He stowed away the remains of his feast in his coat pockets to be eaten on his way back to the root fortress, resolving to kill some other game on the journey, for the use of the little garrison there. He was now, as he knew, not more than ten or twelve miles from his destination, but it was as yet impossible for him to travel. The swamp was full of cypresses, and it is a peculiar habit of these trees to turn their roots straight upward for any distance, from an inch to many feet, and then to bring them straight down again, making what are called cypress knees. These knees are very sharp on top, and sometimes stand not more than a foot apart. Being of all heights, many of them, as Sam knew, were under water now, and these made travelling impossible, even if there had been no quagmires to fall into, as there were. After studying the situation, Sam determined to remain where he was until the water should subside, and then to travel by daylight, at least until he should be out of the swamp and upon high ground again. The waters of the creek subsided much more slowly than they had risen, and Sam remained at the Sycamore Camp, as he called the place, for four days and nights before he thought travelling again practicable.

He then resumed his march, beset by many difficulties. The ground was muddy everywhere, and impassably so in some places. There were many ponds and pools left in the swamp, and these had to be avoided, so that night had already come before he found himself fairly out of the swamp and on the bank of the river, about two miles below the root fortress. He now began to feel all sorts of apprehensions. He had been away eleven days, and he could not help imagining a variety of terrible things which might have happened to his little band during his absence. Presently he saw a great light up the river, and at once the thought flashed into his mind that the Indians had discovered and butchered the boys and Judie, and were now burning the drift pile.

"I'll hurry on," he said to himself, "and if the Indians are really there, it's time for me to take part in this war. I can keep in the timber and pick off half a dozen of them there in the fire light. Then if they scalp me, I don't care. I'll at least make them suffer for what they've done."

A fierce storm was just breaking,—a storm of the violent and heroic type seen only in tropical and sub-tropical countries, but Sam thought nothing of that. He pushed on almost unconsciously, with no thought except that with his rifle, hidden in the darkness, he could wage one sharp and terrible battle with the murderers of Judie and Tom and Joe, before suffering death at their hands. The lightning struck a tree just ahead of him, but he seemed not to observe the fact. He was going into battle, and what was a thunderbolt more or less at such a time. The rain followed, drenching him instantly, but not dampening his determination in the least.

George Cary Eggleston

CHAPTER XII

AN ALARM AND A WELCOME

When Tom and Joe made the disheartening discovery that in spite of all their efforts the fire was burning inside the hammock, they felt like giving up in despair, and seeking another refuge.

"But then Sam would never find us," said Tom, "even if he gets back. He will find this place burned up and think the Indians have killed us all. We *must* put this fire out, Joe, if it takes a week."

And straightway the boys began again, saturating large armfuls of moss with water and laying them on top of the drift whenever the blaze showed itself. Heart-pine burns rapidly with a great blaze and much smoke, but it makes no coals, and a gallon of water will sometimes stop the burning of a great log of it, instantly. Every armful of wet moss therefore had an immediate and perceptible effect which greatly encouraged the boys. They worked hour after hour, not succeeding in putting the fire out, indeed, but managing to check it very decidedly, and better than all, to keep it away from the trees and from the alley-way leading to their hiding-place. Just as night fell, Joe called out,

"I say, Mas' Tommy, it's gwine to rain bucketsful."

"I wish it would," said Tom, looking up to the black clouds which as yet he had hardly observed at all. Just then a sharp flash followed by a sudden peal of thunder almost stunned the boys.

"Dat didn't strike fur from here," said Joe.

"No, it must have hit a tree down the river a little way," said Tom.

The rain followed in torrents, and little Judie came out of her hiding-place to beg the boys to come in lest the lightning should strike them. They were encouraged by the rain, however, to continue fighting the fire, and resumed operations at once.

"Hush!" said Tom presently, "there's Indians about. I heard 'em walking in the brush. Run around the hammock quick, and let's hide."

All ran without a moment's hesitation, and secreting themselves in the drift awaited results.

Presently they heard footsteps in the alley-way, and the voice of their big brother called out.

"Where are all you, little people, and what do do you hide from me for?"

The Indian they had heard was Sam creeping around to see who it was that was burning the drift. Seeing the boys and Judie, he walked out of the thicket, but before he could get to them they had taken refuge in the drift from the supposed danger. Their joy at Sam's return, and Sam's joy at finding them safe and well instead of finding Indians dancing around their burning dwelling, may be imagined. Tom put his arm around his brother's neck, and could say nothing but,

George Cary Eggleston

"Dear old Sam," which he said over again every ten seconds during half an hour at least. Judie hugged and kissed Sam, and cried over him and called him her "dear, best, big brother," and did all sorts of foolish things which didn't strike Sam as foolish at all. Joe would sit awhile and then get up and dance until he knocked his shins against some of the drift, and then set down again, and then get up and dance again, grinning with delight, I have no doubt, though it was too dark for anybody to see whether he grinned or not.

After a little while Sam went out and returning reported that the rain had completely extinguished the fire. They then retired to the root fortress which was unhurt, and Sam said he thought they ought to hold prayers before going to sleep. Sam prayed rather awkwardly perhaps, but he prayed because he felt like thanking the Father who had watched over them all in so many dangers, and the awkwardness of such a prayer is a matter of no consequence. They all laid down, after prayers, and one after another fell asleep.

The next morning a fire was started after the plan Sam had adopted in the swamp, and some game which he had killed made a savory breakfast for all of them. Judie thought salt, which she now tasted for the first time in many weeks, was altogether better than sugar,—an opinion which it seems she never before held. After breakfast explanations were in order. Sam told the others all about his adventures, and they gave him a minute history of their life during his absence. Then Sam explained that from the number of savages he had seen on that side of the river, he thought the other side must now be comparatively free from them.

"Fort Glass is just twelve miles away from here," he said, "and I mean now to go there, just as soon as I get a little rested and feel strong enough. The country along this part of the river is very bad to travel through, though, since the river rose, as all the creeks are up, and if we could get up the river about eight miles, we should be within six miles of the fort, with a good country to travel through. We can't get there, however, and so it's no use to talk about it. We must just strike out from here and make our way across the best way we can."

But clearly Sam was in no condition to travel yet. His fever had come back on him that morning, and it was necessary to postpone the journey to Fort Glass until he should get better. He went into the woods during the day, and shot two squirrels and a wild turkey, but upon his return found himself unable to sit up longer. The bed of scraped moss was very welcome to the weary and sick boy. The next day he was a little better, but the next found him very ill and partly delirious. The boys were frightened. They had seen enough of the fevers of that region to know that they require immediate and constant treatment, and they had good reason to fear that Sam could never recover without medicine and a doctor. They ministered to him as well as they could, but they could do nothing to check the fever, which was now constant and very high. Sam knew hardly anything, and rarely ever spoke at all except to talk incoherently in fits of delirium.

CHAPTER XIII

JOE'S PLAN

Sam's illness continued day after day, and the boys were greatly troubled. Little Judie remained by her "big brother's" side almost constantly, while Tom and Joe provided food, cooked it, and attended to the wants of the little community to the very best of their ability. They were in the habit too, of retiring now and then, to a secluded spot in the drift-pile, to consult and discuss plans of procedure. One day Tom went to the rendezvous and found Joe there leaning against a log, with his feet on another, and his eyes closed.

"Are you asleep, Joe?" he asked.

"No, Mas' Tom, I'se not asleep," said Joe, "I'se just thinkin'."

"Well, what were you thinking, Joe?"

"I'se been layin' plans, Mas' Tom, an' I's laid one good un anyhow."

"What is it, Joe?"

"Well, you see Mas' Sam ought to have a doctor, an' he's gwine to die if he don't, dat's sartain. But dey ain't no doctor here."

Joe said this as if it were a new truth just discovered, that there was no doctor there.

"Well, go on, Joe," said Tom, "and tell me your plan, maybe it's a good one."

"Course it's a good un. I dun tell you dat fust."

"Well, what is it?"

"Mas' Tom, don't you know Mas' Sam always begins 'way back whar' he's been thinkin' an' tells all dat fust so you kin see all de why's and wharfores?"

"Yes; but what has that to do with your plan, Joe?"

"Nothin', only dat's de way I'se gwine to 'splain my plan, I'se dun begun way back whar I'se dun been thinkin', an' I'se gwine to tell all 'bout dat fust. Den you'll understan' de whys and wharfores. You mus'n't hurry me, Mas' Tom, dat's all."

"All right, tell it your own way, Joe," said Tom, laughing.

"No, I'se gwine to tell it Mas' Sam's way. Well, you see dey ain't no doctor here an' we can't git one to come here neither. So we must take Mas' Sam to whar' dey is doctors, do you see?"

"That's all very well," said Tom, "but how are we to do that?"

"Now you'se hurryin' me again, Mas' Tom. Dat's just what I'se a-comin' to. Mas' Sam said de other mornin' dat if we was up de river about eight miles furder, de fort would be only six miles away, an' de country would be easy 'nuff to cross. He dun say we couldn't git up de river, but we *kin*. You see Mas' Sam was sick, an' dat's de reason he say dat.

Now I dun bin thinkin' of a way to git up de river. Dey's lots of cane here, an' you an' me kin twis' canes one over de other like de splits in a cha'r bottom, an' dat way, when we gits a dozen big squars of it made, as big both ways as the canes is long, we kin lay 'em on top o' one an' other, an' fasten 'em togedder wid bamboos, an' it'll be a fust-rate raft. Den you an' me kin pole it up stream, keepin' close to de shore, wid Mas' Sam an' little Miss Judie on it. When we git up dar, I kin go over to de fort, leavin' you wid Mas' Sam till de folks comes after you all."

This was Joe's plan of operations, and upon thinking it over Tom was disposed to think it the best plan possible under the circumstances. Accordingly he and Joe went to work at once. They could not make the raft inside the drift-pile, for want of room, but they found a place in the bushes near the mouth of the creek, where they could work unobserved. They cut down a large number of the flexible green canes, and wove them together into a square net work. Repeating this operation several times they finally had enough of the squares to make, they thought, a secure raft, when laid one on top of the other. It would not do to join them in the bushes however, as that would make their weight so great that the boys could not lift them to the water. They determined, therefore, to get their pushing poles first, and then to carry the squares one by one to the river, and, arranging them there, to embark soon after nightfall. The work of construction had occupied many days, and it was now the 12th of November. The boys hoped to complete their undertaking the next day and embark the next night. After their return to the drift-pile, however, it occurred to Tom to inquire whether or not Joe knew the way from the river to the fort, after they should reach the end of their voyage.

"I 'clar', Mas' Tom, I never thought o' dat at all!" said Joe in consternation. "I dunno a foot of de way, an' I dunno whar' de fort is either."

Tom being equally ignorant, their long consultation held on the spot, ended in an enforced abandonment of the enterprise which had occupied their heads and hands for so long a time.

"Now dar' it is, Mas' Tom," said Joe. "Dat's always the way. Mas' Sam never makes no blunder, 'cause he thinks it all out careful fust. Poor Joe's head gets things all mixed up. I ain't no count anyhow, an' I jest wish I was dead or somethin'."

Poor Joe! The disappointment was a sore one to him. He had been thinking all along of the glory he should reap as the saviour of the little party, and now his whole plan was found to be worthless. He slept little that night, and once Tom heard him quietly sobbing in his corner. Creeping over to him Tom said:

"Don't cry, Joe. You did your best anyhow, and it isn't your fault that you don't know the way to the fort," and passing his arm around the poor black boy's neck he gently drew his head to his shoulder, where it rested while the two slept.

The next morning Judie was the first to wake, and she quietly waked Tom and Joe.

"Boys, boys," she cried in a whisper, "the Indians are all around us, there is a fight going on. Get up quick, but don't make any noise."

The little girl was right. Rifles were cracking and Indians yelling all around their little habitation. It at once occurred to Tom that here was hope as well as danger. If the Indians should be driven back by the whites, he could communicate with the latter and the little garrison of the root fortress would be rescued. At present, however, it was the savages and not the whites who surrounded the trees and the drift pile. Tom determined lose no chance, however, and cautioning the others to keep still, he went to the look-out to watch for an opportunity to communicate with the white men whom these Indians were evidently fighting.

CHAPTER XIV

THE CANOE FIGHT

Before going further with the story of what happened around the root fortress on that morning, it is necessary to explain how it came about that a battle was fought there. I gather the facts from authentic history.

During all the time spent by the Hardwickes in their wanderings and in the root fortress, the war had been going on vigorously. The occupants of Fort Sinquefield, when they abandoned that fort as described in the early chapters of this story, succeeded in making their way to Fort Glass, or Fort Madison, as it was properly named, though the people still used its original name Fort Glass in speaking of it, for which reason I have so called the place throughout this story. In July General Floyd, who was in command of all the United States forces in the south-west, sent General Claiborne, with his twelve months' Mississippi volunteers to Fort Stoddart, with instructions to render such aid as he could to the forts in the surrounding country. His force consisted of seven hundred men, and of them he took five hundred to Fort Stoddart, sending the remaining two hundred, under Col. Joseph E. Carson, a volunteer officer, to Fort Glass. The two hundred soldiers added greatly to the strength of the place, and with the settlers who had taken refuge inside, rendered it reasonably secure against attack. The refugees were under command of Captain Evan Austill, himself a planter of the neighborhood.

Shortly after the storming of Fort Sinquefield, and almost immediately after the garrison of that place had reached Fort Glass, the Indians appeared in great numbers in that neighborhood, burning houses, killing everybody who strayed even a few hundred yards outside the picket gates, and seriously threatening the fort itself. In view of these facts Col. Carson sent a young man of nineteen years of age named Jerry Austill, the son of Capt. Evan Austill to General Claiborne's head-quarters, with dispatches describing the situation and asking for reinforcements. Young Austill made the journey alone and at night, at terrible risk, as he had to pass through a country infested with savages, but on his return brought, instead of assistance, an order for Col. Carson to evacuate the fort and retire to Fort Stephens. When he did so, however, Captain Austill and about fifty other planters, with their families, determined to remain and defend Fort Glass at all hazards. Among those who remained was Mr. Hardwicke, who, now that the Indians had murdered his children, as he supposed, had little to live for, and was disposed to serve the common cause at the most dangerous posts, where every available man was needed.

After a time Col. Carson was sent back to the fort with his Mississippi volunteers, and this freed the daring spirits inside the fort from the necessity of remaining there. They went at once on scouting parties, Tandy Walker, the guide, being almost always one of the number going out on these perilous expeditions. They scoured the country far and near, in bodies ranging from two or three to twenty or thirty men, and fought the Indians in many places, losing some valuable men but making the Indians suffer in their turn.

Finally it was determined to send out a party larger than any that had yet gone, to operate against the savages on the south-east side of the river. This expedition numbered seventy-two men, thirty of whom were Mississippi Yauger men, under a Captain Jones, while the others were volunteers from private life. The expedition was under the command of Sam Dale, already celebrated as an Indian fighter, and known among the Creeks, with whom he had lived, as Sam Thlueco, or Big Sam, on account of his enormous size and strength. During this Creek war he had performed some feats of strength, skill and daring, the memory of which is still preserved in history, together with that of the celebrated canoe fight, which we are now coming to. To tell of these deeds of prowess would lead us away from our proper business, namely, the telling of the present story; but the canoe fight comes properly into the story, being in fact one of its incidents. Three only of Dale's companions figured with him in the canoe fight, and they alone need mentioning by name. These were, first Jerry Austill, the young man already spoken of, who was six feet two inches high, slender but strong, and active as a cat; second, James Smith, a man of firm frame and dauntless spirit; and third Caesar, a negro man, who conducted himself with a courage and coolness fairly entitling him to bear the name of the great Roman warrior.

The expedition left Fort Glass on the 11th of November, 1823. Tandy Walker was its guide, and every man in the party knew that Tandy was not likely to be long in leading them to a place where Indians were plentiful. He knew every inch of country round about, and nothing pleased him so well as a battle in any shape. The day after they left Fort Glass, Dale's men reached the river at a point eighteen miles below the present town of Clairborne, and about fifteen miles below the root fortress. Here they crossed, in two canoes, to the eastern shore of the river, and spent the night without sleep. The next morning Austill, with six men, ascended the river in the canoes, while Dale, with the rest of the party, marched up the bank. About a mile below the root fortress,

Dale who was marching some distance ahead of his men, came upon some Indians at breakfast, and without waiting for his men to come up, shot their chief. The rest fled precipitately, leaving their provisions behind. Pushing on, Dale reached a point about two hundred yards below the root fortress, and there determined to recross the river. The canoes transported the men as rapidly as possible, but when all were over except Dale and eight or nine men (among whom were Smith, Austill and Caesar), and only one canoe remained at the eastern side of the stream, a large party of Indians, numbering, as was afterwards ascertained, nearly three hundred, attacked the handful of whites still remaining. These retreated from the field, where they were breakfasting, and keeping the Indians in check by careful and well-aimed firing, were about to get into the canoe and escape to the opposite bank, about four hundred yards away, when they discovered that their retreat was cut off by a large canoe full of Indians, eleven in all, which had come out of the mouth of the creek just above. The savages tried to approach the shore, but, in spite of the fact that by careening the canoe to one side and lying down they were able to conceal themselves, they were prevented from landing by Austill and one or two other men. Two of the Indians jumped into the water and tried to swim to the shore, while the others, firing over the gunwale of the boat, were sorely annoying the whites. Austill shot one of the swimmers but the other escaped to the shore, and joined the savages there, informing them, as Dale supposed, of the weakness of his force, which they had not yet discovered. Dale called to the men on the other side of the river to cross and assist him, but they, after making an abortive attempt to send a canoe load across, remained idle spectators of the terribly unequal conflict. Dale, seeing that no help was to come from them, and knowing that the Indians would shortly overcome him by sheer force of numbers, resolved upon a recklessly daring manoeuvre, namely, an attempt to capture the Indian canoe! He called out to his comrades.

"I'm going to fight the canoe with a canoe. Who will go with me?"

Austill, Smith and Caesar volunteered at once, and Caesar took his post as steersman, while the three stalwart soldiers were leaping into the canoe for the purpose of fighting hand to hand the nine Indians opposed to them. As they shot out from the shore the savages on the bank delivered a fierce fire upon them, but fortunately without effect. The savages in the canoe had exhausted their powder, and Dale's party would have had an advantage in this but for the fact that their own powder had become wet as they were getting into their canoe. The fight must be hand to hand, but they were not the men to shrink from it. When the boats struck, the Indians leaped up and began using their rifles as clubs. Austill, who was in the bow of Dale's boat, received the first shock of the battle, but Caesar promptly swung his boat around, and grappling the other canoe held the two side by side during the whole fight. Dale's boat was a very small one, and he to relieve it sprang into the Indian canoe, thereby giving his comrades more room and crowding the Indians so closely together as to embarrass their movements. The blows now fell thick and fast. Austill was knocked down into the Indian boat, and an Indian was about to put him to death when Smith saved him by braining the savage. Austill then rose, and snatching a war club from one of the Indians used that instead of his rifle. Eight of the savages were slain, and Dale found himself face to face with the solitary survivor, whom he recognized as a young Muscogee with whom he had been for years on terms of the most intimate friendship, and whom he loved, as he declared, almost as a brother. He lowered his up-raised rifle to spare his friend, but the savage would not accept quarter. He cried out in the Creek language, which Dale understood as well as he did English.

"Big Sam, you are a man, and I am another! Now for it!" and with that the two joined in a struggle for life. A blow from

Dale's gun ended at once the canoe fight and the life of the young brave, who, even from his friend, would not accept the mercy which his nation was not ready to show to the whites. It is said that to the day of his death Dale could not speak of this incident without shedding tears.

Dale and his comrades had still a duty to do and some danger yet to encounter. The party remaining on the bank was in imminent peril, and must be rescued at all hazards. The little canoe was not large enough to carry them all, and so the big one must be cleared of the dead Indians in it, and the heroes of the canoe fight accomplished this under a severe fire from the bank. Then jumping into the captured boat, they paddled to the shore, and taking their hard pressed comrades on board, crossed under fire to the other side, whence they marched to Fort Glass, twelve miles away, having dealt the savages a severe blow without losing a man. Austill was hurt pretty badly on the head, and a permanent dent in his skull attested the narrowness of his escape.

This battle was waged within sight of the root fortress, the drift pile being indeed the cover from which the Indians fought. Tom, as we know, went to the look-out at the beginning of the fight, and he remained there to the end in the hope that the fortune of battle might possibly bring the whites within call, and thus afford the little refugee band a chance of escape. No such chance came, however, and sadly enough the two boys, for Joe was also in the look-out, watched the passage of the last of Dale's men across the stream, half a mile below.

"Mas' Tom," said Joe, "dem folks gwine right straight to de fort."

"Yes, of course," said Tom. "What of it?"

"Nothin', only I wish I could go wid 'em, and tell 'em Mas'

Sam's here sick."

"So do I, Joe, but we can't go with them, and it's no use wishing."

"I reckon 'tain't no use, but I can't help wishin' for all dat. When folk's got der own way dey don't wish for it. It's when you can't git your way dat you wish, ain't it?"

Tom was forced to admit that Joe was right, and that in wishing to be with the retreating party he was not altogether unreasonable.

The two boys sat there, looking and longing. The savages had disappeared almost as suddenly as they had come, and presently Joe sprang up, saying.

"Dar's de little canoe lodged in the bushes, an' I'se gwine to fasten her to the bank anyhow, so's we'll have her if we want her."

What possible use they could make of the canoe, it had not entered Joe's head to ask perhaps, but he tied the boat in the bushes nevertheless and secreted the paddle in the drift pile. He then visited the place where Dale's men had been surprised at breakfast, and brought off the pack of provisions which Dale had captured that morning from the savages and had himself abandoned in his turn. The pack was a well-stored one, and its possession was a matter of no little moment to the boys, whose bill of fare had hitherto embraced no bread, of which there was here an abundance in the shape of ash cake.

"Mas' Tom," said Joe that evening, "do you know my master?"

"Mr. Butler? Yes, certainly."

"Well, if anything happens to poor Joe, and if you ever gits to de fort an' if Joe don't, an' if you sees my master dar you'll tell him Joe never runned away anyhow, won't you."

"Yes, I'll tell him that Joe."

"Even if the Ingins ketches me an' you dunno whar' I'se gone to, you'll tell him anyhow dat Joe never runned away from him or from you nuther, won't you, Mas' Tom?"

"Of course, Joe. But there won't be any chance to tell him anything about it unless we all get back to the fort, and then you can tell him for yourself. He thinks you are dead, of course, and doesn't dream that you ever ran away. You'll get back safely if the Indians don't catch you, and if they catch you they'll catch all of us, so I won't be there to tell your master about you."

"Dun no 'bout dat," replied Joe. "Dey mought catch Joe 'thout catchin' anybody else, an' 'thout you nor nobody knowin' nothin' 'bout it, and Joe wants you to promise anyway dat you'll stick to it to de las' dat poor Joe was no runaway nigger, nohow at all. Kin you do dat for me, Mas' Tom?"

"Certainly, Joe," said Tom laughing, "I promise you."

"Will you git mad if Joe axes you to shake han's on dat, Mas' Tom? I wants to make sartain sure on it."

Tom laughed, but held out his hand, convinced that the poor black boy was out of spirits at least, if not out of his mind.

CHAPTER XV

THE BOYS ARE DRIVEN OUT
OF THE ROOT FORTRESS

Sam was only partially conscious during the battle around his habitation. The fever, which now rose and fell at intervals, was usually highest during the forenoon, abating somewhat later in the day. When it was highest he was always in either an unconscious stupor, or a wild delirium. When the fever abated, however, his consciousness returned, and he was capable of talking and of understanding all that was said. In these lucid intervals, he insisted upon knowing all that had happened, so that he might tell the boys what was best to do. On this day Tom had a story of more than ordinary interest to tell him, about the battle and the chance of rescue which had so narrowly passed them. Sam was interested in it all as a matter of course, but he was still more deeply interested, it seemed, in the condition of the sand near the place where he was lying. He had dug a little hole with his hand, and feeling of the sand found it decidedly wet. Turning to Tom, he said:

"The river is rising rapidly, isn't it?"

"Yes; but how did you find it out?"

"By the sand. I've been watching it a good deal since the fall rains set in, as I'm afraid the river will drive us out of here.

You see, the water works easily through the sand, and you can always tell what the level of the river is, if its banks are sandy, by digging down to where the sand is wet."

"Yes," said Tom, "but the river isn't within a hundred feet of us yet."

"You are mistaken. It is within six inches of us," said Sam.

"How's that?"

"Well, this bank is almost exactly level, and when the river gets above its edge it spreads at once all over it. Now the sand is wet within six inches of the top, and the river is within six inches of the edge of the bank. When it rises six or eight inches more, it'll be in here, and I'm afraid it will rise that much before morning. At any rate we must be ready for it."

"What can we do?" asked Tom in alarm. "There's no place to hide on the upper bank."

"We mustn't quit this bank, and we mustn't quit the drift-pile either," replied Sam. "You must find a good place, high up in the drift where, by pulling out sticks, you and Joe can make a place for us to stay in."

"But, Sam, what if the water gets to us there?"

"It won't get to us there."

"How do you know?"

"Because the biggest freshets always come in the spring, and the top of this drift-pile was put where it is by the biggest freshets, so the river won't go near the top in November. You see, as the drift *floated* on top of the water to its present place, the top of the pile must be the highest point, or very nearly the highest, that the water ever reaches. If you can find a good place therefore in the upper part of the drift-pile, we shall be safe there. But you'd better see about it at once, as the water may be in here before morning, and at any rate we mustn't allow ourselves to be taken by surprise. You'd better go to the river and set a stake first so you can tell how fast the water rises and know when to move into the new place."

Tom set his stake at the water's edge and then selected the most available place he could find for the new abode. He and Joe went diligently to work, rearranging the loose sticks of drift-wood and even carrying many of them clear out of the pile, so as to enlarge the hole they had found and make it as habitable as possible.

"The trouble is," said Tom when they had nearly completed their task, "that we can't make a smooth floor, and it's going to be rather uncomfortable lying on loose logs and big round sticks that run every which way."

"That's my business," said Judie looking in at the entrance. "I'm the housekeeper, you know, and I've thought of all that."

And sure enough the little woman had brought a great pile of small, leafy, tree branches and bush tops, with which she speedily filled up the low places between the timbers, and covered the timbers themselves to a depth of three or four inches, making a soft as well as a level floor. She had foreseen the difficulty, and borrowing Sam's knife, had worked with all her might to provide in advance against it. But the bushes and leaves were not all that she had brought. She had collected also a large quantity of gray moss with which to make a carpet for the springy floor.

"Now please don't tell brother Sam," she said when the boys

George Cary Eggleston

praised her thoughtfulness and ingenuity. "I want to surprise him when he comes."

Tom and Joe promised, and Tom said they would have to call her their "little housekeeper" hereafter.

The river was still rising, but more slowly, it appeared, than it had done before. By Tom's calculations it was coming up at the rate of an inch in three hours, wherefore Sam thought they might safely remain where they were until morning at least, while if the water should come to a stand during the night, they would have no occasion to move at all, as a fall would rapidly follow, if the weather should remain clear.

Joe had worked faithfully at the task of preparing the new place of refuge, but he was not at all satisfied with the arrangement.

"I tell you, Mas' Tom," he said, "wood'll float, 'thout 'tis live oak, an' dis here drif-pile 'll jest raise up an' float away, you'll see if it don't."

"Why hasn't it floated away long ago, then, Joe?" asked Tom.

"May be it has. How you know dis drif' didn't all on it come here las' time de river was up?"

"Well, there's too much of it for that, and besides, Sam says this place is safe, and you know he is always right about things when he speaks positively about them."

"Mas' Tom, don' you know Mas' Sam done been a-talkin' nonsense for two weeks now?"

"Yes; but that's only when he's out of his head."

"How you know when he's outen his head an' when he ain't?"

"We know he's out of his head when he talks nonsense."

"Well, maybe dis here 's nonsense. I jest knows it is, and dat's how I know Mas' Sam was outen his head when he said it."

Tom saw that Joe was not to be convinced, and so he contented himself with saying,

"Well, we'll see."

"Yes, dat's jest it. We *will* see, and feel too, when we all gets drownded in de water."

The water came to a stand about midnight, and was falling slowly the next morning. But when morning came it was raining hard, and the rain was evidently not a local but a general one, wherefore, Tom feared that the fall would shortly be changed into a rise, and that the bank would soon be covered. He watched his stake carefully, visiting it every half hour. At nine o'clock the river had fallen three inches, and was about eight inches below the bank. From nine to ten it fell only about half an inch. Between ten and eleven the fall was not more than a quarter of an inch. Between eleven and twelve no fall at all was perceptible. From twelve to one there was a slight rise. Between one and two it rose nearly an inch. The next hour brought with it a rise of two inches. By five o'clock the level of the water was barely two inches below the edge of the bank, and as it was rising at the rate of two or three inches an hour, Sam thought it time to remove from their old to their new quarters. The change was of advantage to the sick boy, who was now getting somewhat better at any rate, and when he found himself in the new place the interest he showed in examining all the details of its arrangements, was the best possible evidence of improvement.

"Come here, little woman," he said to Judie, "and give an account of yourself. You borrowed my knife yesterday, and somebody has been using it in cutting bush tops to make a smooth floor with, and the idea was a very good one. Can you tell me who it was?"

"Maybe it was Tom," she replied mischievously.

"No, it was not Tom," Sam answered. "He's too much of a great awkward boy to think of anything so comfortable. You must guess again."

"Joe, then," she said.

"No, it wasn't Joe, either," said Sam. "Joe can sleep on the edge of a fence rail as well as anywhere else, and he never would have thought of making our floor soft and smooth. Guess again."

"Maybe it was brother Sam," said Judie.

"Oh, certainly. It must have been I," replied Sam. "I must have done it. I'm so strong and active now-a-days. Yes, on reflection, I presume I did it, and the man in the moon helped me. Now I think it was a very thoughtful and helpful thing for anybody to do, so you ought to kiss me for doing it, and when the weather gets clear you must throw a kiss to the man in the moon, too, for his share." And with that he kissed the little housekeeper, and she felt herself abundantly repaid for her work and for the thoughtfulness she had shown. She was never so happy as when Sam praised her, "because he's such a splendid big brother," she would explain.

Tom, seeing that Sam was getting better at last, began to hope for his complete recovery, and the hope made him buoyant of spirit again. Judie, too, who watched and weighed every symptom in Sam's case, discovered to her delight that he was decidedly better, and the discovery made her as happy as a healthy girl well can be. Poor Joe seemed to be the only miserable one in the party. He said almost nothing, answering questions with a simple "yes" or "no," and sitting moodily in his corner, when he stayed inside the "drift cavern"—which was Sam's name for the new abode—at all. He spent most of his time, however, on top of the pile, where he watched the water and the clouds. The rain had ceased, but the river, which was now creeping over the broad bank, continued to rise.

"What is the matter with Joe?" asked Sam after the boy had gone out for the twentieth time.

"I think he's afraid we're all going to be drowned," said Tom.

"Drowned? How?"

"Well, he says wood will float, and so he thinks when the water comes up under the drift-pile, it will all float away."

"What nonsense!" exclaimed Sam. "Why didn't you tell him better, Tom?"

"I did; but he sticks to it, and—"

"Well, couldn't you explain it so that he would understand it and not have to trust to your judgment for it?"

"No, I couldn't. The fact is, I don't quite understand it myself. There isn't a stick in this whole pile that won't float, and I don't quite understand why the pile won't. But I don't doubt you're right about it, Sam. You always are right whether I understand how things are or not."

"Let me explain it to you, then. Do you know why some things float and others don't?"

"Yes, of course. Because the things that float are lighter than the things that sink."

"Not exactly. That log there is too heavy for you to lift, while you can carry a bullet between your thumb and finger. The log is many hundred times heavier than a bullet, but the log will float while the bullet will sink always."

"That's so," said Tom, "and I don't know what does make some things float and other things sink."

"Did you ever set a teacup in the water and see it float?"

"Yes, many a time."

"But if you fill it with water it will sink, won't it?"

"Yes, of course."

"Well, now I can explain the thing to you, I think. If a thing is heavier,—the whole thing I mean, than the amount of water it displaces,—that is, if it is heavier than exactly its own bulk of water, it will sink; but if it is lighter than its own bulk of water it will float."

"Oh, yes, I see."

"Now a bullet weighs a good deal more than its own bulk of water, and so it sinks. A log weighs less than its own bulk of water, and so it floats. An empty teacup weighs less than a solid body of water equal to it in size, and it therefore floats. If you fill it with water, however, you increase its weight without adding anything to the amount of water it displaces,—or rather, as you let water into all the hollow space, you lessen by that much the amount of water it must displace in sinking without taking away anything from its weight, and so it sinks; or, if you break the teacup you lessen the amount of water it must displace without lessening its weight, and so it sinks in that case, too. Do you understand that?"

"Yes, I think I do," said Tom; "but I don't exactly see how it applies to the drift-pile."

"I'll explain that presently. I want to make it plain first that the ability of a thing to float depends not on its weight, but on its weight as compared with that of a like bulk of water. This comparative or relative weight is called *specific gravity*, and in measuring the specific gravity of substances water is taken as the standard usually, though sometimes gold is used for that purpose. Now to come to the drift-pile. When the water rises say two or three feet, it will be above the level of the lower logs, and these would float away, if they were free, because their specific gravity is less than that of water. But there is twenty feet of other timber on top of them, and its weight must be added to theirs. The water displaced is exactly equal to their bulk, while the weight is many hundred times greater than theirs. Do you understand?"

"Yes, I think I do. You mean that the water must come high enough to pretty nearly cover the whole drift-pile before any of it can float."

"Yes. The pile must be considered as a whole, and it won't float until there is water enough to float the whole. The bottom logs can't float while those above them are clear out of water, if their weight rests on the bottom logs, as it does in the drift-pile. You see when you put anything into the water, it sinks until it has displaced a bulk of water equal to its own weight, and then stops sinking. In other words, that part of the floating thing which goes under the water is exactly the size of a body of water equal in weight to the whole thing. If a log floats with just half of itself above water, you know that the log weighs exactly the same as half its own bulk of water, or, in other words, that its specific gravity is just half that of water. Water two inches deep won't float a great saw-log, because a great saw-log weighs more than the amount of water it takes to cover its lower part two or three inches deep; and water two or three feet deep won't float a drift-pile twenty feet high, because such a drift-pile weighs a good deal more than a body of water two or three feet deep, of its own length and width. But even if the water were to rise to the top of the hammock, the pile wouldn't float away. It would float, of course, and some of the wood near its edges would be carried away, but the main pile would remain here, because it is all tangled together and can't go away except in one great mass. It is so firmly lodged against the trees as to prevent that, and as a freshet big enough to cover, or nearly cover it, would bring down a great quantity of new drift and deposit it here, the pile would grow bigger rather than smaller. But the river won't get very high at this season, or at any rate it won't rise to anywhere near the top of the hammock, as I have already explained to you, because it is evidently only the biggest freshets that ever come near the top, and the biggest freshets never come in the fall, but always in the spring. It isn't rising fast enough either. It isn't rising nearly so fast now as it was before it got over the bank."

"Why, how do you know that, Sam? You haven't been to look."

"No, but I know it, nevertheless, simply because I know that water, left to itself, will find its level."

"I don't see what that's got to do with it," said Tom.

"Perhaps not, but it has something to do with it for all that," replied Sam; "and I can make you see how, too."

He paused, to think the matter over and determine how to present it to Tom's comprehension.

"You see," he then resumed, "that the river inside its banks is about four hundred yards wide. When it rises above the banks, however, it spreads out over the level ground, and becomes, in some places, many miles wide, averaging a mile at least in width. Now there is only a certain amount of water coming into the river every hour. The rain has stopped, but the soil is full of water, and so there is about as much running into the river now as there was while the rain lasted. But the surface of the stream is now many times greater than it was, and as water finds its level, all that comes into the river spreads out over its whole surface, and of course doesn't raise its level nearly so much as the same quantity did while the stream was still within its banks. Do you understand now?"

"What a great big brother you are, Sam, anyhow!" was all the reply Tom made.

CHAPTER XVI

WHERE IS JOE?

It was now getting late, and Sam knew that it was not well for him to talk longer. He felt so much better, however, that he knew he would continue to talk in spite of himself unless the whole party should go to sleep at once. Joe had not been in the drift cavern for more than two hours, and Sam, observing his prolonged absence, said:

"Tom, I'm afraid some of us have hurt poor Joe's feelings. Go and look at your water-mark, and while you are out, find the poor fellow and find out what's the matter with him. He's a good boy, and has done his part faithfully ever since we started. I can't bear to think of him moping."

Tom went out and examined his stake, which showed that the water was not more than an inch or two over the bank, and was not rising very rapidly now; but he could see nothing of Joe anywhere. He went to the look-out, but the boy was not there, and a diligent search through the drift-pile, showed that he was nowhere in the neighborhood of the fortress. Tom was now fairly alarmed, and returning, was about to report the facts to Sam, when little Judie, in a whisper, informed him that the big brother was asleep. As his fever had risen somewhat, Judie rightly thought it better not to disturb him, as he certainly could not aid in any way in finding Joe.

"I must just think," Tom said to himself, "as Sam does, and then I can do all there is to be done. Now I know Joe isn't anywhere in the hammock, because I knew every place he could squeeze himself into, and I've looked in every one of them. It's no use then to waste time looking there any more. He must have left here, either accidentally or on purpose. He couldn't have slipped off the drift and drowned, because he can swim pretty well and would have swam out in a minute. There is no other way in which he can have left here by accident, unless an Indian has killed him on the drift-pile somewhere, and if that were so I would have found his body. He must have run away on purpose."

But just as Tom reached this point in his thinking he remembered the earnestness with which poor Joe had begged him to bear witness in any and every event that he was not "a runaway nigger." And this reminded Tom of all the queer ways he had noticed in Joe of late. The boy must have had a premonition, he thought, that something was going to happen to him. Only two theories remained. One was that Joe had gone crazy under his long exile from civilized life and had madly put an end to himself by jumping into the river; and the other that, persisting in his belief in the instability of the drift-pile, he had gone to the upper bank for safety and had fallen asleep there. In that event he must be found, lest an Indian should discover him in the morning and put him to death. Tom went ashore after explaining his purpose to Judie, so that she might not be alarmed at his absence, and literally spent the entire night in hunting for the black boy. Joe was nowhere to be found, and when daylight came, Tom saw that a further search was of no use whatever, and he therefore returned sadly to the drift cavern. The water was now going down again, and the bank was free from it, but the sand in the root fortress was still too wet to sit or lie upon, and so Tom made no immediate preparation for their return.

Sam's fever was very slight that morning, and his first question was about Joe. Tom told him of his night's search, and Sam's deduction from all the facts was that the poor boy had committed suicide, had been killed by an Indian and thrown into the river, or had fallen in accidentally and drowned.

"He would never have left us in any case," said Sam, "and even had he been less faithful, he would have been afraid to run away, not knowing where to run or how to take care of himself in the woods."

They were too much grieved for Joe's loss, to relish their breakfast, and that meal was dispatched very quickly. Tom watched the falling of the water all day, and at night reported that the river was well inside its banks again.

CHAPTER XVII

A FAMINE

The river having gone down until no water remained on the sandy bank, Tom reported the fact and added,

"Now let's move back again to the root-fortress. It's a safer place than this, by a good deal, if it isn't quite so big or quite so comfortable."

"No, we mustn't go back yet," said Judie, who had visited the fortress before Tom had, "because the sand in there is as wet as can be, and I can't let my big sick brother lie on it."

"There, Tom," said Sam, "my doctor forbids my return yet awhile, and a sick man always must obey the doctor you know. Besides, Judie is right. It won't do for any of us to lie on wet sand; we must wait till it dries; but that won't be very long if the river continues to go down."

Accordingly they spent one more night in the drift cavern. Early the next morning Judie went to the fortress, and returning said, playing doctor.

"Now, then, Mr. Hardwicke, the floor of your lower house is quite dry, and I think it will be safe to move back again. Will you have your breakfast first, or will you wait until you get back home again before eating anything?"

"Oh, let's wait, by all means, and eat breakfast in the dear old root-fortress," said Tom, and as Sam made no objection, it was so arranged.

By nine o'clock the moss carpet was laid in the root-fortress and the little party was back in its old quarters again. The vacant corner which had been Joe's, reminded them sadly of his disappearance. Poor fellow! they had learned to love him almost as a brother, and they could not think of him now without tears. When three people sit down with a silent grief, their conversation is very apt to be lively, or, if they cannot quite accomplish that, they are sure to talk only of indifferent matters, and so it was in the present case. Judie was the first to break the silence which had fallen upon all.

"Tom," she said playfully, "I'm afraid you're not a good provider. Here we are, hungry as wolves, and you haven't brought us a mite of anything to eat. You've moved everything but the provisions, and you've forgotten them entirely."

Master Tom admitted the grievousness of his fault and returned at once to the drift cavern after the forgotten provision pack. The bread, as they all knew, was long ago exhausted, but plenty of meat remained, and this Tom presently brought. When he opened the pack a disagreeable odor spread itself at once over the little room.

"Phew! what's that?" said Tom, and putting his nose to the meat, he looked up in blank consternation, saying:

"The meat is spoiled, Sam! What on earth shall we do?"

The case was an alarming one certainly. They were hungry, and Sam, whose returning health had brought with it a

ravenous appetite, was particularly so. He needed wholesome, nourishing food now more than anything else, as he
knew.

"Well," he said, after thinking the matter over, "it can't be
helped. There's nothing for it but to fall back on sweet
potatoes till I get strong enough to go hunting. You must go
to the potato field Tom, and bring some."

There had been but one field of corn in the neighborhood at
first, and the various parties of Indians who had camped in
its vicinity had long ago carried away the last ear of corn
from that, as the boys knew very well. The river was
altogether too high now for mussels to be got, and so the
sweet potatoes in a field half a mile away, were their only
resource.

Tom set out at once in quest of them, carefully looking out
for lurking savages. He was gone more than an hour, and just
as Sam was growing really uneasy on his account, he
returned, *empty handed*!

"There isn't a potato in the field," he said as he sat down in
utter dejection. "The Indians have dug every one of them."

This announcement was indeed an alarming one to the whole
party. They were without an ounce of food of any sort within
their utmost reach, and it was plain that they must starve,
unless they could hit upon some new device, by which to get
a supply.

"I must go hunting, sick or well," said Sam rising; but he had
no sooner got upon his feet, than he felt the utter impossi-
bility of doing anything of the kind.

"It's of no use," he said sadly. "I can't make my legs carry
me, Tom, and so we must depend upon you. Go into the

woods there by the creek, and sit down or stand still till you see something in the way of game, and then take good aim before you shoot, for we mustn't waste any of our powder."

With this he shook the horn to ascertain how much remained in it, and was horrified to find it empty! Tom remembered that the last time he had loaded the gun he had used the last grain of powder in the horn.

"Well, then," said Sam, "we have only one charge of powder between us and starvation, and it won't do to waste that, Tom. You can shoot pretty well when you have time enough to take good aim, and I suppose, if you make up your mind beforehand that you won't shoot till you know you can kill what you shoot at, it is safe enough. At any rate we must risk it. Remember, however, that you mustn't run the risk of wasting this load in your anxiety to kill the first thing you see to shoot at. There is plenty of game in the woods, so if you can't get a sure shot at one thing, wait for another. Get a sure shot anyhow, if it takes you all day. It must be something big enough to last us awhile, too. You mustn't shoot at anything less than a turkey or a 'possum, and you mustn't shoot at all till you get *very* close, because if you miss, we will starve. Better take all day to-day and all day to-morrow than to miss when you fire."

And after many instructions and cautionings, Tom sallied forth in search of game. Going into the woods for a considerable distance, he sat down on a log in the thick undergrowth and waited patiently for the appearance of some animal which could be eaten. Hour after hour passed, and Tom fell asleep. How long he slept he did not know, but waking suddenly he saw a flock of wild turkeys within a few yards of him. Raising his gun and taking a very deliberate aim he pulled the trigger. No explosion followed, but the clicking of the hammer was enough to put the game to flight.

Poor Tom was disheartened, but it would not do to give up, and so he carefully picked the edge of his flint with his knife and walked further into the woods.

He had not walked very far, with cautious steps, when he heard a rustling in the bushes just ahead of him. At first he thought it must be an Indian, and drawing back he waited for further developments. A grunt soon enlightened him as to the character of the game, and creeping through the bushes he found himself close to a fat young hog, one of the many running wild in those woods and thickets. That was something worth having. Levelling his gun again, he again pulled the trigger, but without effect, and opening the pan he discovered that during the rain, while in the drift cavern, the "priming," as the powder in the pan is called, had been reduced to a paste by water. To fire the gun was out of the question, and so clubbing it, Tom ran at the hog and dealt him a blow on the head, hoping in that way to secure the game which he could not shoot. The blow fell upon the nose of the animal, however, and while it brought a squeal of pain from him, it produced no beneficial result. The hog ran rapidly away, and Tom was left with nothing better than a broken gun to carry back to the fortress.

Arriving there about three o'clock in the afternoon he told the doleful story of his failure, and sitting down burst into tears.

"Come, come!" said Sam. "This will never do, old fellow. It's bad enough as it is without crying about it. We'll come all right if you'll only keep your courage up, and give me a chance to think. I'm getting better every day now, and if we can only hold out a few days longer, I'll be on my feet again, and then we'll go straight to Fort Glass. Just as soon as I can walk at all, we'll start, meantime we must get something to eat, and to do that I must think. Let me see. The gun is of no use now, but there are other ways of getting game besides shooting it. We must set some traps. This spoiled meat will do for bait. Get me a good piece of poplar wood, Tom, or cypress, or some other sort, that I can whittle easily, and I'll make some figure-four triggers. Then I'll tell you how to make dead-falls, and you must set as many of them as you can to make sure of getting something to eat by to-morrow morning."

Tom brought the wood and Sam soon whittled out several sets of triggers.

"Now do you know how to set a trap with these triggers, Tom?" he asked.

"Yes, I've set many a partridge trap with figure fours."

"Very well then. Now you must set dead-falls in the same way. That is, instead of a trap you must set a log. You see I've made the triggers big and strong, and you must put them under one end of as heavy a log as you can lift. Then you must lay other logs on top to make it as heavy as possible, and bait it with a piece of the spoilt meat. If anything undertakes to eat the meat to-night, the dead-fall will break its neck or back, sure. Here are six sets of triggers and you must set six dead-falls. We can go hungry till to-morrow, can't we, little woman?" chucking Judie under the chin.

"We can try, anyhow," answered the little woman as cheerfully as she could, though she was by no means confident that she could do anything of the sort. She was already faint and almost sick, and whether she could live till morning or not was an undetermined question in her mind. To tell the truth, Sam himself felt but little confidence in his device. The spoiled meat, he knew, would attract only the larger animals, and such dead-falls as Tom could set were by no means certain to kill these in their fall. It was the very best thing he could do, however, and he must trust to it in the absence of any better reliance. He concealed his anxiety therefore, and after receiving Tom's report of his operations in dead-fall setting, he drew Judie to his side and told her a fairy story, as night fell. All went to sleep at last, and when morning came Sam aroused Tom very early and sent him to examine the traps. The boy was gone for an hour or more, when he returned with downcast countenance. Two of the traps had been thrown, but there was no game under them, while the four others remained undisturbed.

Here was a bad out-look certainly, and they had not tasted food now for more than thirty hours!

CHAPTER XVIII

WHICH ENDS THE STORY

"Something must be done," said Sam, as soon as he had heard Tom's report, "and quickly too. Let me think a few minutes. We are beginning now to be hungry enough to eat anything, and when people get that hungry there are a good many things that can be eaten. I'll tell you what we must do, Tom—"

But what it was that Sam had hit upon, Tom never knew. Just as this point in the conversation was reached *Joe* came running in through the alley-way, his face flattened out into a broad grin of delight, his teeth and eyes shining, while he danced all over the fortress, shaking hands over and over again, and saying,

"Hi! Miss Judie! Hi! Mas' Tom! Hi! Mas' Sam! How does ye all do now? Did you think Joe had runned away? Joe tell ye he never runned away. Joe ain't no runaway nigger, nohow at all, and de Ingins ain't ketched Joe nuther. Joe's back all safe an' sound, sartin sure! Hi!"

"What on earth ails you, Joe? You're out of your wits, poor fellow," said Sam, convinced that the black boy was demented.

"No I ain't nuther, Mas' Sam," he replied. "Joe ain't crazy one bit, but he's glad *sure*."

"Where have you been, Joe, since you left us?"

"Whar? Why to de fort, an' I'se dun brung back a rescue too, didn't I tell you? Laws a massy, dat's what I comed in fust for to tell you. I'se done been to Fort Glass and brung a big rescue party, and de white folks dey said, long as Joe brung us he's 'titled to tell de good news fust, an' dat's how I'm here while de rest is outside de drif'."

"Go and see, Tom," said Sam, afraid to believe this story of the seemingly insane boy, who, he thought, had become crazed from long brooding over the chances of rescue. Tom got up to go, but as he started Mr. Hardwicke himself met him in the door way and caught him in his arms. Tandy Walker was just behind.

"Well, this beats all," said Tandy. "I've done a good many jobs o' rescuin' in my time, but I never yit found the rescued hid in the roots of a tree an' fortified with a drift-pile. An' if I'm a jedge o' sich things, this here party's a'most starved. I've seed hungry people afore now, an' I say le's have a breakfast sot right away for these here little ones."

Tandy was right, as we know, and it was not long before an abundant breakfast was spread for Sam and Tom and little Judie. The rescue party consisted of twenty stout fellows from the fort, and after breakfast a rude litter was provided for Sam, and crossing the river in the little canoe the party began its homeward march. Tom was glad to walk, the walk being in that direction. Judie was carried, part of the time in her father's arms, part of it in Tandy Walker's, and part on the broad shoulders of Caesar, the negro man who had participated in the canoe fight. Sam was stretched on a litter, carried by four of the men, and Joe insisted on walking always by his side, though he fell behind now and then for the purpose of dancing a little jig of delight. He would execute this movement, and then running, catch up with the litter again.

"Tell me, Joe," said Sam after the black boy had become somewhat quiet again, "tell me all about this thing."

"'Bout what thing, Mas' Sam?"

"About your going to the fort and all that. How did you manage it, and how came you to think of it?"

"Well, you see, Mas' Sam, when you was at your wust, I got a thinkin', an' I thought out a plan dat Mas' Tom said was a good un. Him an' me was to make a raf' out'n cane, an' pole it up de river wid you an' little Miss Judie on it, an' den I was to go cross de country to de fort an' bring help. Jes' as we got de raf' ready, howsomever, Mas' Tom he axed me if I know de way to de fort, an' as I didn't know nothin' 'bout it, I jis' sot down an' gived up. But I kep' a thinkin' all de time, an' I said to myself, 'Joe, you're a fool anyhow, an' you mustn't tell your plans till you know dey're good uns, an' you ain't got sense enough to know dat till you try 'em.'"

An' so I sot my head to work to git up a new plan, meanin' to try it all by myself. When de big fight took place an' I seed the white folks marchin' away, I said out 'loud, 'dem dare folks is gwine right straight to de fort,' an' I said to myself, 'I means to go dere too if I kin.' It took me two days 'n more to git de thing fixed up right in my min'.

"I was willin' enough to risk Injuns, but I was afear'd you'n Mas' Tom 'ud think Joe was a runaway nigger if I never comed back, an' dat troubled me. I fixed dat at las' by makin' Mas' Tom mos' swar he'd stick to it dat I wasn't no runaway nigger, an' den I sot out. I crossed de river in de little canoe an' hid her in de bushes. I found de place whar de white folks started from, an' I jes' follered dere trail. Dat was my plan. I know'd dey would make a big easy trail, dere was so many of 'em, an I meant to follow 'em. It took me more'n two whole nights to git to de fort, dough, 'cause de creeks was all high an' de brush very tangley. When I tole de folks about you'n Miss Judie an' Mas' Tom, dey didn't more'n half believe me, an' when I tole 'em I'd lead 'em straight to whar you was, an' dey said dey'd sculp me if I didn't, I jest said all right, 'cause if we don' find Mas' Sam an' little Miss Judie an' Mas' Tom no more, den I'd rather be sculped'n not, anyhow. But we did fin' you, didn't we Mas' Sam?" and at this Joe had to drop behind again and execute a rapid jig movement, as a relief to his feelings.

* * * * *

The government forces under General Jackson, together with the settlers themselves, were now pressing the savages very hard. Battles were fought almost every day, and every battle weakened the Indians. In December, General Claiborne invaded the Holy Ground, and utterly destroyed Weatherford's command, as a result of which that chief surrendered to Jackson and the war was practically at an end. A few more battles were necessary before a final peace could be made, and the last of them was fought on the 27th of March, 1814, at Horseshoe Bend; but after the battle of December 23d a little more than a month after Sam's party was rescued, the country north and west of the Alabama river was comparatively free from savages, who no longer dared wander about in small bands, plundering and burning houses, and the planters began to return to their homes to get ready for spring work.

When Mr. Hardwicke was about to go home with his children, he sent for Joe. When the boy came, little Judie handed him a carefully folded document, saying,

"Here's a present for you, Joe."

"What's dis?" asked Joe, unable to guess what possible use he could have for such a paper as that, inasmuch as he couldn't read it to save his life.

"These are your *free papers*, Joe," said Sam. "Father has bought you from Mr. Butler, for the purpose of setting you free, as a reward for your good conduct."

Joe evidently wanted to say something, but did not know how.

"Are you glad to be free, Joe?" asked Mr. Hardwicke.

"Ain't I though?" and Joe's feet began to shuffle as if a jig were coming in spite of his desire to behave well.

"Well, Joe," said Mr. Hardwicke, "I mean to give you a fair chance in life, and I've thought the matter over carefully. You are free now to do precisely as you please, and you can live where you like. But I've a proposition to make—a plan for you. Do you know my cypress farm,—the little one down in the fork of the two creeks?"

"De one whar' ole uncle Peter Dun lived so long?"

"Yes, the one uncle Peter manages for me."

"Yes, master, I knows dat place mighty well."

"Well, how would you like to buy it, Joe?"

"Buy the farm, master? What's Joe got to buy wid? I ain't got no money, 'thout it's a quarter Mas' Tandy Walker dun gim me fur to clean his boots sence we comed back to de fort, an' I jest know that a quarter won't buy no sich low grounds as dem dar down twix' dem dar creeks is. Dat's de very bes' lan' in Alabama. Leastways I dun hear de folks say 'tis heaps o' times. You's jokin' wid Joe, master."

"No, I am not, Joe. You can buy the land if you want it, and there are a hundred and ten acres in the tract, besides the strip of woods along both creeks."

"How's I gwine to buy it, master?"

"Well, let me see. You're about thirteen now. It will be nine years yet before you will be a man, and if you choose to live with me until you are twenty-one, I'll feed and clothe you till then, and the day you are twenty-one the farm shall be yours in payment of wages."

"How you mean, master?"

"I mean, that besides feeding and clothing you as I feed and clothe my people, I will give you the farm for your nine years' work. If you like the place, I will have all the papers made out, so that the farm will be yours, even if I should die before the time is up. I have more land than I care to keep, and you see I want to sell that one farm to you, if you'll buy it."

"Looks to me, heap more like's if you was gwine to give it to me, master; dis on'y your fun to say I buy's it."

"No, the bargain is a fair one, Joe. I could give you the farm now, but I think it will be better for you to work for it, and then you'll feel that it's yours by right and not by favor. I want to make a man of you, Joe, and my children shall always think of you as one of their best friends. Go out of doors if you want to dance, Joe," seeing the feet beginning to shuffle, and understanding the mingled joy and embarrassment of the boy.

Joe hesitated a moment, and then with a sudden straightening of his shoulders, as if the future manliness were already beginning to assert itself in him, he advanced to Mr. Hardwicke, and shaking his hand, said:

"Joe ain't got no learnin' an' no manners nuther, master, but Joe's *grateful* anyhow," and bursting into tears the boy left the room.

THE END

Choose from Thousands of 1stWorldLibrary Classics By

A. M. Barnard	Booth Tarkington	Edward Everett Hale
Ada Leverson	Boyd Cable	Edward J. O'Biren
Adolphus William Ward	Bram Stoker	Edward S. Ellis
Aesop	C. Collodi	Edwin L. Arnold
Agatha Christie	C. E. Orr	Eleanor Atkins
Alexander Aaronsohn	C. M. Ingleby	Eleanor Hallowell Abbott
Alexander Kielland	Carolyn Wells	Eliot Gregory
Alexandre Dumas	Catherine Parr Traill	Elizabeth Gaskell
Alfred Gatty	Charles A. Eastman	Elizabeth McCracken
Alfred Ollivant	Charles Amory Beach	Elizabeth Von Arnim
Alice Duer Miller	Charles Dickens	Ellem Key
Alice Turner Curtis	Charles Dudley Warner	Emerson Hough
Alice Dunbar	Charles Farrar Browne	Emilie F. Carlen
Allen Chapman	Charles Ives	Emily Bronte
Alleyne Ireland	Charles Kingsley	Emily Dickinson
Ambrose Bierce	Charles Klein	Enid Bagnold
Amelia E. Barr	Charles Hanson Towne	Enilor Macartney Lane
Amory H. Bradford	Charles Lathrop Pack	Erasmus W. Jones
Andrew Lang	Charles Romyn Dake	Ernie Howard Pie
Andrew McFarland Davis	Charles Whibley	Ethel May Dell
Andy Adams	Charles Willing Beale	Ethel Turner
Angela Brazil	Charlotte M. Braeme	Ethel Watts Mumford
Anna Alice Chapin	Charlotte M. Yonge	Eugene Sue
Anna Sewell	Charlotte Perkins Stetson	Eugenie Foa
Annie Besant	Clair W. Hayes	Eugene Wood
Annie Hamilton Donnell	Clarence Day Jr.	Eustace Hale Ball
Annie Payson Call	Clarence E. Mulford	Evelyn Everett-green
Annie Roe Carr	Clemence Housman	Everard Cotes
Annonaymous	Confucius	F. H. Cheley
Anton Chekhov	Coningsby Dawson	F. J. Cross
Archibald Lee Fletcher	Cornelis DeWitt Wilcox	F. Marion Crawford
Arnold Bennett	Cyril Burleigh	Fannie E. Newberry
Arthur C. Benson	D. H. Lawrence	Federick Austin Ogg
Arthur Conan Doyle	Daniel Defoe	Ferdinand Ossendowski
Arthur M. Winfield	David Garnett	Fergus Hume
Arthur Ransome	Dinah Craik	Florence A. Kilpatrick
Arthur Schnitzler	Don Carlos Janes	Fremont B. Deering
Arthur Train	Donald Keyhoe	Francis Bacon
Atticus	Dorothy Kilner	Francis Darwin
B.H. Baden-Powell	Dougan Clark	Frances Hodgson Burnett
B. M. Bower	Douglas Fairbanks	Frances Parkinson Keyes
B. C. Chatterjee	E. Nesbit	Frank Gee Patchin
Baroness Emmuska Orczy	E. P. Roe	Frank Harris
Baroness Orczy	E. Phillips Oppenheim	Frank Jewett Mather
Basil King	E. S. Brooks	Frank L. Packard
Bayard Taylor	Earl Barnes	Frank V. Webster
Ben Macomber	Edgar Rice Burroughs	Frederic Stewart Isham
Bertha Muzzy Bower	Edith Van Dyne	Frederick Trevor Hill
Bjornstjerne Bjornson	Edith Wharton	Frederick Winslow Taylor

Friedrich Kerst
Friedrich Nietzsche
Fyodor Dostoyevsky
G.A. Henty
G.K. Chesterton
Gabrielle E. Jackson
Garrett P. Serviss
Gaston Leroux
George A. Warren
George Ade
Geroge Bernard Shaw
George Cary Eggleston
George Durston
George Ebers
George Eliot
George Gissing
George MacDonald
George Meredith
George Orwell
George Sylvester Viereck
George Tucker
George W. Cable
George Wharton James
Gertrude Atherton
Gordon Casserly
Grace E. King
Grace Gallatin
Grace Greenwood
Grant Allen
Guillermo A. Sherwell
Gulielma Zollinger
Gustav Flaubert
H. A. Cody
H. B. Irving
H.C. Bailey
H. G. Wells
H. H. Munro
H. Irving Hancock
H. R. Naylor
H. Rider Haggard
H. W. C. Davis
Haldeman Julius
Hall Caine
Hamilton Wright Mabie
Hans Christian Andersen
Harold Avery
Harold McGrath
Harriet Beecher Stowe
Harry Castlemon
Harry Coghill
Harry Houidini

Hayden Carruth
Helent Hunt Jackson
Helen Nicolay
Hendrik Conscience
Hendy David Thoreau
Henri Barbusse
Henrik Ibsen
Henry Adams
Henry Ford
Henry Frost
Henry James
Henry Jones Ford
Henry Seton Merriman
Henry W Longfellow
Herbert A. Giles
Herbert Carter
Herbert N. Casson
Herman Hesse
Hildegard G. Frey
Homer
Honore De Balzac
Horace B. Day
Horace Walpole
Horatio Alger Jr.
Howard Pyle
Howard R. Garis
Hugh Lofting
Hugh Walpole
Humphry Ward
Ian Maclaren
Inez Haynes Gillmore
Irving Bacheller
Isabel Cecilia Williams
Isabel Hornibrook
Israel Abrahams
Ivan Turgenev
J.G.Austin
J. Henri Fabre
J. M. Barrie
J. M. Walsh
J. Macdonald Oxley
J. R. Miller
J. S. Fletcher
J. S. Knowles
J. Storer Clouston
J. W. Duffield
Jack London
Jacob Abbott
James Allen
James Andrews
James Baldwin

James Branch Cabell
James DeMille
James Joyce
James Lane Allen
James Lane Allen
James Oliver Curwood
James Oppenheim
James Otis
James R. Driscoll
Jane Abbott
Jane Austen
Jane L. Stewart
Janet Aldridge
Jens Peter Jacobsen
Jerome K. Jerome
Jessie Graham Flower
John Buchan
John Burroughs
John Cournos
John F. Kennedy
John Gay
John Glasworthy
John Habberton
John Joy Bell
John Kendrick Bangs
John Milton
John Philip Sousa
John Taintor Foote
Jonas Lauritz Idemil Lie
Jonathan Swift
Joseph A. Altsheler
Joseph Carey
Joseph Conrad
Joseph E. Badger Jr
Joseph Hergesheimer
Joseph Jacobs
Jules Vernes
Julian Hawthrone
Julie A Lippmann
Justin Huntly McCarthy
Kakuzo Okakura
Karle Wilson Baker
Kate Chopin
Kenneth Grahame
Kenneth McGaffey
Kate Langley Bosher
Kate Langley Bosher
Katherine Cecil Thurston
Katherine Stokes
L. A. Abbot
L. T. Meade

L. Frank Baum	Owen Johnson	Stephen Crane
Latta Griswold	P.G. Wodehouse	Stewart Edward White
Laura Dent Crane	Paul and Mabel Thorne	Stijn Streuvels
Laura Lee Hope	Paul G. Tomlinson	Swami Abhedananda
Laurence Housman	Paul Severing	Swami Parmananda
Lawrence Beasley	Percy Brebner	T. S. Ackland
Leo Tolstoy	Percy Keese Fitzhugh	T. S. Arthur
Leonid Andreyev	Peter B. Kyne	The Princess Der Ling
Lewis Carroll	Plato	Thomas A. Janvier
Lewis Sperry Chafer	Quincy Allen	Thomas A Kempis
Lilian Bell	R. Derby Holmes	Thomas Anderton
Lloyd Osbourne	R. L. Stevenson	Thomas Bailey Aldrich
Louis Hughes	R. S. Ball	Thomas Bulfinch
Louis Joseph Vance	Rabindranath Tagore	Thomas De Quincey
Louis Tracy	Rahul Alvares	Thomas Dixon
Louisa May Alcott	Ralph Bonehill	Thomas H. Huxley
Lucy Fitch Perkins	Ralph Henry Barbour	Thomas Hardy
Lucy Maud Montgomery	Ralph Victor	Thomas More
Luther Benson	Ralph Waldo Emmerson	Thornton W. Burgess
Lydia Miller Middleton	Rene Descartes	U. S. Grant
Lyndon Orr	Ray Cummings	Upton Sinclair
M. Corvus	Rex Beach	Valentine Williams
M. H. Adams	Rex E. Beach	Various Authors
Margaret E. Sangster	Richard Harding Davis	Vaughan Kester
Margret Howth	Richard Jefferies	Victor Appleton
Margaret Vandercook	Richard Le Gallienne	Victor G. Durham
Margaret W. Hungerford	Robert Barr	Victoria Cross
Margret Penrose	Robert Frost	Virginia Woolf
Maria Edgeworth	Robert Gordon Anderson	Wadsworth Camp
Maria Thompson Daviess	Robert L. Drake	Walter Camp
Mariano Azuela	Robert Lansing	Walter Scott
Marion Polk Angellotti	Robert Lynd	Washington Irving
Mark Overton	Robert Michael Ballantyne	Wilbur Lawton
Mark Twain	Robert W. Chambers	Wilkie Collins
Mary Austin	Rosa Nouchette Carey	Willa Cather
Mary Catherine Crowley	Rudyard Kipling	Willard F. Baker
Mary Cole	Saint Augustine	William Dean Howells
Mary Hastings Bradley	Samuel B. Allison	William le Queux
Mary Roberts Rinehart	Samuel Hopkins Adams	W. Makepeace Thackeray
Mary Rowlandson	Sarah Bernhardt	William W. Walter
M. Wollstonecraft Shelley	Sarah C. Hallowell	William Shakespeare
Maud Lindsay	Selma Lagerlof	Winston Churchill
Max Beerbohm	Sherwood Anderson	Yei Theodora Ozaki
Myra Kelly	Sigmund Freud	Yogi Ramacharaka
Nathaniel Hawthrone	Standish O'Grady	Young E. Allison
Nicolo Machiavelli	Stanley Weyman	Zane Grey
O. F. Walton	Stella Benson	
Oscar Wilde	Stella M. Francis